D1541544

Finding the Hidden Self

Ex Libris

George & Wanda
Lysloff

Finding the Hidden Self

A Study of the Śiva Sūtras

Roger Worthington, Ph.D.

Himalayan Institute Press
Honesdale, Pennsylvania

The Himalayan Institute Press
RR 1, Box 1129
Honesdale, PA 18431

© 2002 Roger Worthington

All rights reserved. No part of this book may be reproduced in any form or by any means without permission in writing from the publisher. Printed in the United States of America.

First printing

Cover design by Michele Wetherbee
Page design by Joan Gazdik Gillner

Library of Congress Cataloging-in-Publication Data

Worthington, Roger.
Finding the hidden self: a study of the Siva Sutras / Roger Worthington.
p. cm.
Includes bibliographical references and index.
ISBN 0-89389-185-1 (pb: alk. paper)
1. Vasugupta. âívasâtra. 2. Kashmir Saivism--Doctrines. I. Vasugupta. Sivasutra. English and Sanskrit. II. Title.

BL1281.1592.V38 A2765 2001
294.5'95--dc21 2001024911

To Pārvatananda

CONTENTS

ACKNOWLEDGMENTS

I was first drawn to begin studying the *Śiva Sūtras* in the late 1980s, and in the course of doing a new translation and writing this commentary I received help, advice and encouragement from several kind and learned people. The first was Jeanine Miller, a friend and an accomplished Vedic scholar, who provided the impetus to begin writing this book, as well as the great benefit of her wisdom. I also thank two distinguished teachers, Śri Mathoor Krishnamurti (now Executive Director of Bharatiya Vidya Bhavan, Bangalore) and Śri B. B. Konnur (Pāṇduranga), for their kindness and support.

While this book is not written as a work of comparative philosophy, it deals with a set of ideas that are attracting comment in the West, albeit from a different perspective. The Eastern spiritual tradition is very rich, and I believe it has much to offer students of philosophy, especially on this question of consciousness. The original sūtras are less well known than other ancient Indian texts, and few editions as yet have appeared in English. I am familiar with four in total—one by Śrinivasa Iyengar, serialized between 1907 and 1909, another by I. K. Taimni, published in 1976, and a third by Jaideva Singh, which appeared in 1979, all of which originated in India.

Finally, there is the translation by Mark Dyczowski, 1992 (USA), which is primarily a translation of Bhāskara's commentary, the Vārttika. This work adds greatly to the scholarship attaching to Kaśmiri Śaivism.

When I came to the U.S. in 1998 I was pleased to have the opportunity to meet Śri Rajmani Tigunait, pandit, and spiritual director of the Himalayan International Institute, and the Institute has honored me in accepting this work for publication. I hope the readers will share my love of this text, and will gain something, not just from my labors in writing and translating, but from the labors of all those who have helped to make this project come to fruition.

The Spelling and Pronunciation of Sanskrit Letters and Words

Sanskrit vowels are generally the same pure vowel sounds found in Italian, Spanish, or French. The consonants are generally pronounced as in English.

a	org*a*n, s*u*m
ā	f*a*ther
ai	*ai*sle
au	s*au*erkr*au*t
b	*b*ut
bh	a*bh*or
c	*ch*ur*ch*
ḍ	*d*ough
d	*d*ough (slightly toward the *th* sound of *th*ough)
ḍh	a*dh*ere
dh	a*dh*ere (slightly toward the *theh* sound of brea*the h*ere)
e	pr*e*y
g	*g*o
gh	do*gh*ouse
ḥ	[slight aspiration of preceding vowel]
h	*h*ot
i	*i*t
ī	pol*i*ce
j	*j*ump
jh	lod*geh*ouse
k	*k*id
kh	wor*kh*orse
ḷ	no English equivalent; a short vowel pronounced somewhat like the *lry* in revelry

l	*l*ug
ṃ or ṁ	[resonant nasalization of preceding vowel]
m	*m*ud
ṅ	si*ng*
ṇ	u*n*der
ñ	pi*ñ*ata
n	*n*o
o	n*o*
p	*p*ub
ph	u*ph*ill
ṛ	no English equivalent; a simple vowel *r*, such as appears in many Slavonic languages
ṝ	the same pronunciation as ṛ, more prolonged
r	*r*um
ś	*sh*awl (pronounce with a slight whistle; German *sp*rechen)
ṣ	*sh*un
s	*s*un
ṭ	*t*omato
t	wa*t*er
ṭh	an*th*ill
th	*Th*ailand
u	p*u*sh
ū	r*u*de
v	*v*odka (midway between w and v)
y	*y*es

Vowels. Every vowel is either long or short. The diphthongs *e, o, ai,* and *au* are always long; *ḷ* is always short. Long *a, i,* and *u* are indicated by a horizontal line over the vowel. The long form of a vowel is pronounced twice as long as the short form.

Consonants. Sanskrit has many aspirated consonants, that is, consonants pronounced with a slight *h* sound: *bh ch ḍh dh gh jh kh ph ṭh th.* These aspirated consonants should be pronounced distinctly. The retroflex consonants, *ḍ ḍh ṇ ṣ ṭ ṭh,* are pronounced with a hitting sound, as the tip of the tongue is curled back to the ridge of the hard palate. The dentals, *d dh n t th,* are pronounced with the tip of the tongue touching the upper teeth.

Accentuation. There is no strong accentuation of syllables. The general rule is to stress the next-to-last syllable of a word, if that is long. A syllable is long if *(a)* it has a long vowel or *(b)* its vowel is followed by more than one consonant. If the next-to-last syllable is short, then the syllable before that receives the stress.

Introduction

An attempt has been made in this book to uncover some of the mysteries contained in the verses, or ślokas, known as the *Śiva Sūtras*. This book started from a deep spirit of inquiry into the nature of mind and consciousness, and while the translation from the Sanskrit is as accurate as possible, the main emphasis has been placed on the underlying philosophy. Many Western philosophers have searched hard for the elusive entity called consciousness, but nowhere has it been captured better than in these sūtras, which simply speak of how things are, and not of suppositions. There is little intellectual, speculative thinking in classical Indian philosophy, because it stems from the realm of direct experience. But such experience is what in the West would be called "intuitive," and as such it is partly outside of normal, everyday conscious activity. Hence these sūtras may require a certain act of faith on the part of the reader, but such faith should not be blind, and it is my hope that the reader will recognize the profound nature of this text and increasingly realize the living truth contained within it. I have tried to preserve the inner qualities of the original, while making it accessible to present-day English-speaking readers.

The verses are a good subject for meditation, and can perhaps best be understood in this way. Some readers will be familiar with other literature on the philosophy of yoga composed in the form of sūtras, such as the *Yoga Sūtras* of Patanjali. These can serve as a useful preparation or supplement to the *Śiva Sūtras*, and it is necessary from the beginning to understand the essential characteristics of this aphoristic form of teaching. A sūtra is a condensed verse, and is usually an incomplete sentence. The text is composed of sūtras strung one after another after another. The main reason for this compositional technique is that short phrases are easier to remember. These aphorisms are part of the oral tradition of spiritual teaching, whereby knowledge has been passed on from guru to disciple—sometimes for thousands of years—without the need for writing. Aphorisms are not verses in the normal literary sense, but are phrases which encapsulate an idea or a particular aspect of a teaching. The teacher is then expected to elaborate and comment on the text as part of the method of instruction.

Translating aphorisms is therefore a process of reconstruction, requiring knowledge not merely of the language but of the underlying teaching. This reconstruction can lead to variations of interpretation; hence it is necessary always to supply the original Sanskrit ślokas or sūtras. *Śloka* is the more general term, and can be used to refer to any sacred verse or hymn. The word *sūtra* literally means "thread": sūtras are threads of words that are woven together to clothe a living body of thought that is itself a conceptual image of an underlying spiritual reality that is beyond words.

The *Śiva Sūtras* describe the creative principle which is behind the whole manifested universe, in relation to the evolving nature of human consciousness. The origin of the *Sūtras* is mysterious; legend has it that they were discovered engraved on a large tablet of stone by Vasugupta, on the Mahādeva Mountain (Mount Kailas) in Kaśmir. Vasugupta was said to have been guided by Lord Śiva in a dream to the spot where the stone lay, and these *Sūtras* are regarded by many as a divine revelation. They constitute one of the two main texts of Kaśmiri Śaivism. (The other main text is the *Pratya-bhijñā-hṛdaya [The Secret of Self-Realization].*) Śaivism, which is the practice of devotion to the Lord Śiva, is an ancient practice and is part of the Hindu tradition. Śiva is worshipped as the Supreme Being, and is here revered as the creator, preserver and destroyer of the universe. However, in other Hindu texts Brahma and Viṣṇu are given the roles of creator and preserver, respectively.

Śiva has countless manifestations, and accordingly, in Vedic and post-Vedic literature Śiva is referred to by many different names, of which 108 are most sacred and used in daily prayers of devotion. (Over a thousand names for Śiva are given in the *Liṅga Purāṇas,* although these are of later origin.) It is important to remember that Lord Śiva is primarily worshipped through mantra. The best-known mantra, "Oṃ namaḥ Śivāyaḥ," or *pañcakṣari* ("the five-syllabled mantra"), is recited by the devotee countless times, in the conviction that by the japa (constant repetition) of a mantra its power is increased.

In Śaivite literature Śiva and his consort appear in different forms and are known by different names. For readers without a knowledge of Hindu mythology this may be confusing, and the aim here has been to strive for simplicity, in relation to both the text and the commentary. The *Śiva Sūtras* are central to the Śaivite religion, but it is not within the compass of this work to delve into the symbolism and mythology. Śiva, Īśvara and Maheśvara are essentially different names for one and the same being. While Pārvatī is one of many names given to the consort of Śiva, reference is made in this work only to Śakti, whose power is synonymous with the universal Divine Mother.

The Lord Śiva is worshipped by all Hindus, and the tradition of revering this aspect of the deity reaches back to before the beginning of recorded history. Vasugupta founded the first major school of Śaivite philosophy in the mid-ninth century A.D. Kśemarāja, a pupil of Abhinavagupta (an eleventh-century Śaivite scholar and philosopher), was writing somewhat later. Kśemarāja was the author of the *Pratya-bhijñā-hṛdaya,* and wrote a commentary on the *Śiva Sūtras* known as the *Śivasūtra-vimarśinī*. This commentary is familiar to devotees, and has been an authoritative commentary ever since it was first written, roughly a thousand years ago.

The history of the *Sūtras* is really not so important as their contents: that is, their insights into the nature of mind and consciousness.[1] The vastness of scope and the profundity of the *Sūtras* is awe-inspiring, and encompasses the whole of the creative energy that manifests in every form in the universe.

---

1. Readers interested in reading more about the origin and history of the *Śiva Sūtras* are recommended to read the two works by Mark Dyczkowski listed in the bibliography.

The *Śiva Sūtras* are divided into three parts, or "books." Book One, *Śāmbhavopāya,* which comprises 22 sūtras, has been said to correspond with the jñāna-yoga of the *Bhagavad Gītā.* It concerns the supreme divine state, or the creative spirit of the universe, which is present in every being. It describes the way towards realization of the Divine, and towards the realization of Śakti, or that power of the Divine which is within. Some commentators consider it the most important part of the teaching, as it deals with the successive states of consciousness and with the nature of ātmā itself.

Book Two, *Śāktopāya,* which comprises only 10 sūtras, is concerned with mantra-yoga. It relates to the supreme divine powers, of which mantra is an outward expression. These powers are derived from the union of citta and ātmā, and sound (in its purest form) is employed as the vehicle of expression.

Book Three, *Āṇavopāya,* is the largest in terms of size and scope, and comprises 45 sūtras. It describes the philosophy and understanding behind aṣṭāṅga-yoga ("eight-limbed yoga"); it concerns itself with the nature of the Divine Consciousness and with the constituent elements of the universe. In samādhi (a state of absorption and bliss) these elements are transformed as the yogi enters the higher states of consciousness. Turīya (the fourth state of consciousness, beyond waking, dreaming and sleeping) acts as the vehicle or mode of transformation.

The *Śiva Sūtras* are unquestionably demanding, containing as they do a comprehensive spiritual realization in a most compact form. But it is hoped that the reader who greets this challenge will find the experience deeply rewarding.

Book One

Śāmbhavopāya: The Realization of Śiva

Sūtra 1.1

चैतन्यमात्मा ।

caitanyam-ātmā

Ātmā is of the nature of pure consciousness.

Pure consciousness, which is essentially self-luminous, *is* ātmā. The first sūtra makes a short statement which is of profound importance, and it requires more contemplation than formal commentary. The relationship between consciousness, ātmā and knowledge is a central theme in the whole text and will arise on several occasions.

Sūtra 1.2

ज्ञानं बन्धः ।

jñānaṃ bandhaḥ

Ordinary knowledge is bound by the world of illusion.

Ātmā cannot really be defined, because it is a universal principle and not an object. Consciousness, which is in essence without limitation, is both pure and absolute. The indissoluble link between ātmā and consciousness is at the root of the whole philosophy behind the *Śiva Sūtras*. Ātmā is that spark of pure spirit which is forever part of the Universal Flame, which is itself the source of all life and power. It is present in every being, and nothing that has life is without it.

Ātmā has been described as "the jewel in the lotus"; that is, as something of beauty, hidden from view, except to those who can find the center of "the thousand-petaled lotus."[2] Anything which belongs to the manifested, or phenomenal, world is clothed in a form of many layers, each of which in man separates the mind, or lower self, from the spirit, which is the Higher Self. Consciousness, it will be seen, has different states, and in all but the highest state it is veiled in illusion, and thus ordi-

2. These analogies allude to the fact that *(a)* the flower of the lotus rises above the water, and hence is distinct from all other plants in the water (i.e., all ordinary entities), and *(b)* the thousand-petaled lotus is the familiar name given to the crown cakra, situated on top of the head, and it forms the highest vortex of spiritual energy in the body.

narily prevents the reasoning mind from perceiving the Inner Reality.

Thought is always limited and jñāna, as ordinary knowledge, by definition cannot be absolute. Mind cannot perceive its own true nature except through meditation or through being in that state of luminosity which is the goal of all yoga practice. The very process of involution binds mind (manas) to its vehicle of manifestation, and the human form does not ordinarily respond to vibrations of the higher mind, unless it is trained to do so. What must be firmly established is that the potential for spiritual growth is present in every human being, on account of that spark which is the source of all life, and which is hidden in the center of our being. That spark finds expression only through purity of consciousness; the method for lifting the veil of illusion and penetrating the layers of obscuration is described by Patanjali in the *Yoga Sūtras,* and forms the basis of Raja Yoga.

The *Śiva Sūtras* are concerned with the nature of that consciousness, which is untouched by knowledge and reasoning, and which must be discovered in the innermost part of our being.

Sūtra 1.3

योनिवर्गः कलाशरीरम् ।

yoni-vargaḥ kalā-śarīram

The cause of existence, the type of being and the vehicle of consciousness determine ordinary knowledge, which is itself the source of bondage.

Ordinary knowledge limits the perception of reality. In the *Yoga Sūtras* the modifications of the mind are described, and in this text there is a chance to examine the limitations of knowledge and the cause of bondage.

Manas (mind) is the vehicle of consciousness, and in ordinary waking consciousness it is normally occupied by thoughts and memories, and is not free to function as an instrument of communication with the spiritual Self, or higher mind. The ability for manas to function is therefore influenced by the contents of the mind in ordinary waking consciousness. Truth, which is without distinction, is unaffected by thought or knowledge; it has its own absolute existence, which is entirely independent of perception. Ordinary knowledge, however, is always conditioned, and is limited by numerous factors.

The cause of existence and the type or category of being are also fundamental limitations. If one starts with the supposition that the whole purpose of existence, of birth and rebirth, is for spiritual evolution, then, unless one has attained the status of a bodhisattva and *chooses* to incarnate for the sake of humanity, reincarnation is a spiritual necessity. In other words, the cause of existence and category of being, in terms of evolutionary development, arise from imperfection and the present inability to attain the goal of Liberation.

Sūtra 1.4

ज्ञानाधिष्ठानं मातृका ।

jñānādhiṣṭhānaṃ mātṛkā

The subtle basis of all ordinary knowledge lies in the nature and properties of sound.

Something is revealed here which is of profound importance. Modern physicists have discovered the link between matter and energy, and the spectrum has been found to extend from invisible light rays, at one end, to inaudible sound waves at the other. The common element is *vibration.* Energy is a force which vibrates and which sustains all forms of life. All matter has this energy, but the rate of vibration varies from form to form. In minerals the vibration is extremely slow, and hence mineral objects take a long time to form and have an immensely long life. The rate of vibration which sustains plants is considerably faster than in minerals, and plants have the capability of responding to a number of different stimuli. The animal kingdom is still further evolved, and many of its members are capable of rapid and complex physical movement. In some of the higher species of the animal kingdom creatures are to be found with well-developed brains, and these animals form the next link in the evolutionary chain.

Man stands at the top of the tree of evolution, and the one thing which marks him above all other forms is his highly evolved mental faculties. Thoughts which are produced by the mind have a certain objectivity, and we are told by the Teachers of the Ancients that thoughts leave a permanent impression upon the etheric substance of space (ākāśa). It can be said, therefore, that thought has objectivity, and that its form is a type of a vibration. It is this vibration which is picked up between sensitives who can read each other's thoughts over distance in telepathic communication. Thought waves vibrate, but below the threshold of sensory perception. Essentially, thought is a vibration of the mind, and knowledge is the product of thought, memory and accumulated experience. It may now be imagined how the basis of knowledge is described as having the nature and properties of sound.

Sūtra 1.5

उद्यमो भैरवः ।

udyamo bhairavaḥ

The energy which is to be found in the manifested world is rooted in space (ākāśa), and is an expression of the power aspect of Śiva.

Śiva is the symbol of both creation and destruction. He is the power aspect of the Logos, which is present in every atom of the universe; there is no living particle which is not sustained by the Will of Śiva. The meaning of this sūtra should now become clear, since ākāśa (space) fills the universe and all space vibrates in harmony with the consciousness of Śiva. The primordial essence of all manifestation rests in ākāśa. Ākāśa contains the vital energy, or great breath of prāṇa, from which every living entity draws life. The energy and power of Śiva are absolute and without limitation. However, at the end of the cycle of manifestation the Will is withdrawn, and after a long period of evolution the planet enters pralaya, which is that state of eternal rest known as "a night in the life of Brahma." Nonetheless, in this prolonged silence Śiva remains ever wakeful, while all else sleeps. It is the planet or the universe that enters pralaya and not the Supreme Being, and *power* does not diminish when the Will is withdrawn, it only ceases to interact with matter.

Sūtra 1.6

शक्तिचक्रसंधाने विश्वसंहारः ।

śakti-cakra-saṃdhāne viśva-saṃhāraḥ

Meditation on the Supreme Light of Consciousness brings union with the Divine Energy of Śiva. The power aspect of Śiva, which is everywhere, brings enlightenment to the yogi whose mind is inward-turned.

This sūtra conceals a fundamental principle about the relationship between the noumenal and phenomenal, or unmanifest and manifested, worlds. There is a point of union where the spiritual and material worlds meet. The apparent duality between these two worlds is not real, because they co-exist; they are merely different aspects of the One Truth, where Śiva and Śakti unite. In physical terms, this means that the crown cakra (or Śiva cakra) and the base cakra (or Śakti cakra) form a union, and the circulation of energy through the nāḍīs (hidden channels) is wholly unimpeded.

The noumenal world of the unmanifest is, in esoteric science, the real world, because it is the world of causes and ideation, from which creation springs. The phenomenal world of manifestations is, by contrast, the world of shadows, or of illusions, because it is only a projection in space of the Will of Śiva. That Will is the creative power of the universe, and is the source of light from which are cast the shadows of men on "the moving screen of life." Through meditation the point of communication is reached where conscious union with the source of all power is achieved. The yogi who achieves union with the Higher Self passes through this point, or center, and so pierces the veil of illusion.

Sūtra 1.7

जाग्रत्स्वप्नसुषुप्तभेदे तुर्याभोगसंभवः ।

jāgrat-svapna-suṣupta-bhede turyā-bhoga-saṃbhavaḥ

The fourth state of consciousness is experienced by piercing through the states of waking consciousness, the dream state and the state of dreamless sleep, in blissful awareness of the true nature of reality.

This sūtra expands upon the previous one by listing the ordinary states of consciousness and describing the possibility of transcending the limitations of ordinary consciousness.

Ordinary waking consciousness is familiar to us as the constant chattering of the mind. This can be controlled through the practice of meditation, which stimulates an awareness of the true nature of Reality. The dream state is characterized by illusion, since all manner of astral forms play upon the rational mind when it is not in control of the thinking process. Dreamless sleep is not a state of spirituality, since consciousness has not transcended the rational thinking process. Consciousness is only temporarily without means of communication with the ordinary, rational mind in dreamless sleep. This state is beneficial and restful to mind and body, but has nothing to do with samādhi, or realization of the ātmā.

Sūtra 1.8

ज्ञानं जागृत् ।

jñānaṃ jāgrat

Knowledge gained in the wakeful state of consciousness (jāgrat) is by direct contact between mind and object.

The various states of consciousness are now examined in turn. This sūtra is fairly explicit, and although the means of contact between mind and object will vary, perception may be by any or all of the five senses (indriyas), after which memory is employed to identify the object. In the process of identification, the mind sifts through data stored in the memory, and then rational thought evaluates the information before a response is made. Sometimes no action is necessary, but at other times a reaction is required, which might need to be extremely fast. Reactions to sensations of touch, for example, are instinctive and bypass the thinking process completely, by the transmission of electrical nerve impulses. The process of responding to sound, however, is more subtle, and hearing is the most highly evolved of all the senses.

Sense experience, whether pleasant or painful, is neither spiritual nor creative. It is of value in everyday living, but must be assigned to its proper place. Because sense experience is rooted in the world of manifestation, it is both temporary and illusory, and in order that the higher states of consciousness may dawn, all such experience must be transcended. Jāgrat may be perceived simply as the concentration of the mind upon an object, but such knowledge can also be derived by means of inference, or by the testimony of others, without engaging the senses.

Sūtra 1.9

स्वप्नो विकल्पाः ।

svapno vikalpāḥ

The dream state (svapna) is that in which mental activity is independent of contact with the objective world.

Svapna is the dream state in which the mind draws its material from planes of existence devoid of objectivity. The contact between mind and object, discussed in the previous sūtra, is missing, and the mind is occupied by impressions drawn from the astral plane. The impressions or abstract forms which mold our consciousness in the dream state appear as real as any impressions in the waking state, but in fact they are quite illusory in nature.

Memory is again a key factor in producing the forms which

project onto the screen of consciousness during sleep; however, the possibility of impressions drawn from outside the limits of personal experience needs to be considered. Modern psychology speaks of the "collective unconscious"; it is possible that when individual consciousness is in the dream state, and is aware only of astral forms, some of these forms may be drawn from the collective unconscious. When mixed with forms derived from subjective experience, they mingle to create the chaotic impressions associated with the dream state. Impressions drawn from the astral plane are outside the time-space continuum, which normally renders dreams incomprehensible to the mind that is perceiving them.

The dream state lies between ordinary waking consciousness and the state of dreamless sleep. Dreams which occupy the unconscious mind leave little or no impression on the conscious mind. The experience of dreaming is like that of spectating, in which the mind is observing, but the senses are not engaged. *Some* impressions may filter through into waking consciousness, and be saved by the memory, and while dreams are not founded upon Reality, that is not to say they have no significance. The interpretation of dreams has been given importance since ancient times, and references to this are found in various scriptures. The dream state provides a link with the subconscious, and its essential feature is the absence of ordinary constraints which apply in waking consciousness regarding time, space and motion.

Projections from the past and the future can combine in a disorderly fashion, because the mind is a spectator in the dream state rather than the instigator of conscious thought. Dreams have all the appearance of reality during sleep, but imagination and subconscious impressions determine the actual content of the dream, while contact between the mind and senses is suspended. However, it is said that belief in a possible sequence of events can allow such a sequence to be enacted in the dream state before it assumes a more physical reality. This allows for the possibility of having prophetic dreams.

Dreaming is an important activity during which a variety of impressions and experiences are absorbed. Just as the mind is generally unaware of food once it has passed into the stomach, so the mind needs time to "digest" impressions and experiences from the senses, *(a)* in order to prevent mental strain, and *(b)* to allow impressions to be received which are independent of the physical senses. It is precisely in this state that dreams have such an important role to play.

Sūtra 1.10

अविवेको मायासौषुप्तम् ।

aviveko māyā-sauṣuptam

Dreamless sleep (suṣupti) is characterized by illusion and lack of discrimination.

In dreamless sleep the spirit of consciousness is removed one step further from the plane of objectivity, and in this state there are no means of remembering, or recording impressions. Consciousness is suspended, as it were, between the phenomenal and the noumenal, or the manifest and the unmanifested states. The mind and body are at rest, but consciousness does not cease to exist; rather it operates on other planes. However, because dreamless sleep is an unconscious state of being, the state of dreamless sleep remains illusory in nature. In samādhi there is conscious union between the knower and the known; in suṣupti there is a lack of union, and hence a lack of awareness of the Higher Self. However, while the mind is unable to receive impressions, the ātmā is able to function freely in the world of pure spirit, unhindered by the normal limitations of time and space.

Sūtra 1.11

त्रितयभोक्ता वीरेशः ।

tritaya-bhoktā vīreśaḥ

When these three states merge in a state of bliss, great powers can be exercised on the plane of manifestation.

Sutras 8, 9 and 10 describe the different states of consciousness; in number 11, the results are considered of expanding consciousness until the three ordinary states merge (i.e., the wakeful state, the dream state and the state of dreamless sleep).[3] The powers of Śiva are well known to the Hindu, and reference is found here to the powers that the yogi may attain in pursuing the path of Self-realization. In Book Three of the *Yoga Sūtras* there is an account of some of the siddhis (phenomenal powers) which may be acquired. However, the powers are not in themselves significant and confer no spirituality on the person who possesses them—but they *are* of practical use to the yogi, since they can increase the capacity for accomplishment.

---

3. In content, this sūtra follows on from number 7.

Sūtra 1.12

विस्मयो योगभूमिकाः ।

vismayo yoga-bhūmikāḥ

A sense of wonderment accompanies the various states and stages of accomplishment in yoga.

The path of yoga is not an easy one to follow, and effort is expended in the constant practice of discrimination and dispassion (viveka and vairāgya). Awareness of the true nature of Reality needs to be continuous if consciousness is to rise above ordinary levels of being. In pursuit of this, individual consciousness gradually expands towards a state of conscious union with the Divine, until the spirit is freed from the path of sorrow and suffering which normally afflicts humanity.

One notes from the various states and stages of accomplishment that the process of spiritual evolution is generally slow and difficult, and even the yogi who consciously tries to control his own destiny is unlikely to attain Self-realization all at once.[4] Nonetheless, visions may be experienced along the path, which cause wonderment and a sense of bliss, and this state is accompanied by a sense of inner peace. All activities of the mind cease as the spirit is afforded a glimpse of the world of beauty and truth, which exists not in the imagination of men but as the essential Reality, which normally one lacks the power to perceive.

---

4. Patanjali concedes that there are exceptions to this rule, and it is possible for enlightenment to be spontaneous, when all the circumstances are right.

Direct experience of this state changes one's perceptions, and by recollection and reflection on the state of transformation, a feeling of bliss (ananda) is induced.

Sūtra 1.13

इच्छाशक्तिरुमा कुमारी ।

icchāśaktir-umā kumārī

The willpower of the yogi is of great strength, though not truly infinite, unless wedded with that which is inherent in the consciousness of Śiva.

It is time now to address the question of "Who is Śiva?" or even "What is Śiva?" Any description or definition will necessarily fail, because of the impossibility of using language, which is conditioned by thought, to explain a concept or state of being wholly beyond the limitations of thought. However, Śiva may be described as a deity, or Supreme Being, encompassing the powers of creation, destruction and regeneration. There is no contradiction here between these three characteristics, because creation begins in space from nothing (the eternal void), and only when there is destruction and death can there be regeneration and new life. This common law is readily observed in the rhythms of Nature. The powers of destruction are not wanton, but rather have the attributes of purification and cleansing, and are followed by new life and regeneration.

The history of mankind, in terms of the phases of ancient

civilizations, bears testimony to this cycle of events.[5] Nothing in manifestation is ever permanent. The powers of Śiva are absolute, but in order for the yogi to draw on the great reservoir of strength inherent in the consciousness of the Divine, there must be perfect union between the mind-consciousness of the yogi and the state of unmanifest perfection inherent in the consciousness of Śiva. It is the power of Will (icchāśakti) which is instrumental in effecting this state of union, as the yogi draws closer towards the One Supreme Being.

Sūtra 1.14

दृश्यं शरीरम् ।

dṛśyaṃ śarīram

The objective world is an expansion of the physical body.

The visible objective world includes everything in the field of manifestation, and no distinction need be made between dense physical objects and the images of thought. The physical form is a living part of the process of creation, in which all division is ultimately false. The separateness between one man and another, the duality between the seer and the seen, and all types of

5. "Evidence" of these civilizations is hard to find, but occult records are said to exist, and to be hidden in secret places on the Earth. While the modern historian has every reason to be skeptical of such claims, reference is made by a number of great seers to the existence of these records. Some of them are buried, it has been said, deep in the Himālaya Mountains, and others beneath the desert in parts of the Middle East.

distinction and division are found to be false once the yogi has passed beyond the limitations of ordinary consciousness and become wedded to that infinite source of power encompassed by the Will of Śiva. It can be understood that, to the yogi, the physical body is little more than a vesture which may be cast aside. This vesture serves a useful, not to say invaluable, purpose, but problems arise when an individual mistakes the vesture for that which it is designed to cover.

Identification with the physical form, and with the personality that employs it, is universal, and is a cause of endless human suffering. Such mistaken identity gives rise to the illusion of separateness, and causes man to live in ignorance of the true nature of the self. The yogi who has learnt to employ the light of intuition knows not only the falseness of distinctions and divisions, but knows for himself the essential oneness of all existence. His consciousness, being in union with Śiva, has expanded and taken in the whole world of manifestation. The spirit of ātmā, of which his own consciousness is but a tiny portion, is without limitation, and just as his spirit is part of the universal consciousness, so his body, which is a specialized concurrence of atoms, is not fundamentally separate from any other object or being. In working from the center outwards, the objective world will be perceived as an expansion of the physical body.

Sūtra 1.15

हृदये चित्तसंघट्टाद् दृश्यस्वापदर्शनम् ।

hṛdaye citta-saṃghaṭṭād dṛśya-svāpa-darśanam

Conscious perception of the dreamlike nature of the objective world arises from interaction of the heart and mind.

Until the heart and mind meet and interact, there can be no conscious enlightenment. Mind is the seat of consciousness, and unless it is touched by love and purity of emotion, it is unable to transcend individual limitations. The mind is an instrument of perception, but it is infinitely capable of expansion, and can go beyond the confines of sensory input and conditioned thought. It has to become aware of its inner nature and spiritual capacity, and the yogis teach that this will not happen by effort alone, unless the mind is touched by the inspiring quality of love; in other words, by a meeting of both heart and mind. Furthermore, it should be understood that the physical organs of the heart and the brain have only symbolic meaning in the present context.

Consciousness has many aspects or dimensions, although individual consciousness is normally limited to the actual content of the mind. This content should not be like a straw in the wind, blown in all directions by sensory input, thoughts and memories; rather it should be under the control of the Will. Thoughts may be selected by the mind, but these too may be worthless without the guiding inspiration of the heart. When mind and heart are wedded, a source of great beauty and an ability to perceive the true nature of reality arise, by which conscious perception of the dreamlike character of the whole world of manifestation is known. The objective world of phenomena is not the world of truth, but is a vehicle of evolutionary consciousness (i.e., a vehicle for the Will of the Divine, which is Śiva).

Sūtra 1.16

शुद्धतत्त्वसंधानाद्वाऽपशुशक्तिः ।

śuddha-tattva-saṃdhānādvā'paśu-śaktiḥ

By focusing the attention on the One Reality (or Great Point), the individuality is freed from the binding nature of worldly existence.

The means of crossing the gap between ordinary worldly existence on the material plane and conscious existence on the spiritual plane is described in this sūtra. The Great Point (mahābindu) may be imagined as the center of a lens through which consciousness passes when stripped of its materialism. Once it has passed through that point like a ray of light, then it is possible for the yogi to describe what is on the other side. On one side of the lens is the ocean of worldly existence (saṃsāra), which is the world of the known, and on the other is to be found the ocean of spirituality, or pure being (bhāvanā), which is beyond the scope of the ordinary imagination. What is possible, though, and ultimately essential, is to learn to pass through the lens, or to cross the gap between the worldly and spiritual modes of existence, while wearing the human vesture. Therefore, nirvāṇa is to be experienced in this life and not the next. Self-knowledge, or awareness of the One Reality, is attained by the highest meditation on that Great Point. Intellect alone is not enough to pierce the veil which masks our true spiritual nature.

Meditation on the One Reality is the way to transcend the limitations of ordinary existence and win freedom from the illusions of saṃsāra. The One Reality is pure consciousness and universal, and is without attributes and distinctions of any kind. The secrets of life are not necessarily to be found in some faraway place—in a monastery, or on top of the Himālaya Mountains—but in the recesses of the human heart, in perfect union with the mind, through silent contemplation. Environment may help or hinder the process of achieving spiritual union with the Divine, and daily meditation is not easy in an environment which is noisy, or generally unsuitable, but enlightenment is not restricted to places of physical beauty. In other words, tranquility of mind is the first essential, but enlightenment is a state of being, not a physical location, the most beautiful of which may easily be destroyed by one's own thoughts and emotions, as well as by outside disturbance.

Sūtra 1.17

वितर्क आत्मज्ञानम् ।

vitarka ātma-jñānam

Self-knowledge arises from continuous reflection on the ātmā.

Ātmā is that absolute quality which is truth; it is that Inner Self which is unconditioned and absolute—the jewel within the lotus. It is indestructible and intangible, and Self-knowledge arises when the mind is continuously directed towards the ātmā.

Ātmā and Brahma are in essence the same. They are the spirit of Universal Consciousness which exists in every atom, and yet can never be found with microscopes, computers or anything else put together by man. Methods for suspending the normal processes of the mind are likely to fail when they differentiate between the method and the goal. The method and the goal are one, and that oneness is a state of being (bhāvanā). When the mind occupies that space beyond the confines of the brain, it is capable of perceiving at a level of consciousness which knows no time.[6] The present is then the only

6. The relationship between mind, brain and consciousness has caused problems for so many Western philosophers, and yet in the philosophy of yoga it is clearly set out. The brain is a *vehicle* of the mind, and hence the brain is primarily a physical organ. The mind is an attribute of consciousness, and consciousness (ātmā) is universal. In other words, the brain only *reflects* the true spirit of consciousness, which is within each human being. This a pivotal point of departure between Eastern and Western philosophers, and to believe that consciousness is somehow a function or

reality; love is the strongest emotion and Self-knowledge the greatest achievement. Such are the fruits of the knowledge of ātmā; they will not develop from an occasional application of the will, only from continuous reflection on the spiritual nature of all existence.

Sūtra 1.18

लोकानन्दः समाधिसुखम् ।

lokānandaḥ samādhi-sukham

Eternal bliss can be experienced by focusing the Inner Light on that aspect of the One Reality which is bliss.

Sat-cit-ananda (or pure being, mind, and bliss) are the three aspects of the One Reality. If bliss is to be experienced in waking consciousness, then it must become the object or seed of meditation. The Inner Light, in other words, becomes focused on that aspect of the eternal which is bliss (ananda). Pure or eternal bliss, having been absorbed by the higher consciousness, then fills the mind of the yogi and radiates outward, through space, in the manifested world.

This sūtra describes the practice of meditation in which all

---

attribute of the brain is to "put the cart before the horse." The metaphor of the chariot and the charioteer is used in classical Indian philosophy, the chariot being the vehicle (brain) and the charioteer, the driver (mind). Consciousness is described as a sea or ocean (and hence is universal), and each individual person is but one droplet of water, or to use a different metaphor, a spark from the Universal Flame.

energy is focused on "that aspect of the One Reality which is bliss." In this highest state of meditation (samādhi) the mind exceeds its normal limitations, becoming conscious on the spiritual plane, while absorbed in the experience of Pure Bliss. In samādhi the self as a separate entity ceases to function, and the total union of mind and consciousness gives rise to supreme bliss, which is an essential aspect of the One Reality.

"The Inner Light, or luminosity, is a reference to spiritual well-being, when all the vehicles are working in perfect harmony; this experience of inner peace will bring all modifications of the mind to a halt during meditation, and so strengthen control of the mind in ordinary waking consciousness."[7] The Inner Light is that spiritual luminosity which emanates, in physical form, from the crown of the head.

---

7. This description, taken from *A Student's Companion to Patanjali* [Roger Worthington, Theosophical Publishing House, London, 1987], was written to explain the reference to the Inner Light in *Yoga Sūtras 1:36*, and I believe it is helpful in the present context.

Sūtra 1.19

शक्तिसंधााने शरीरोत्पत्तिः ।

śakti-saṃdhāne śarīrotpattiḥ

Knowledge of the creation of all bodies arises from meditation on and union with the Divine Power, which is the source of the manifested universe.

Here the object of meditation is the union between ātmā and the Divine Power, from which all creation springs. It is said that ātmā and the power of the Divine are essentially the same. If the Divine Power is the source of the manifested universe, then by the practice of meditation (saṃdhāna) on that power, the yogi may come to understand the nature of all creation. The implication, therefore, is that the yogi is capable of forming, or transforming, the elements in a manifested state by the practice of spiritual alchemy. Such power, which could so easily be misused, is only likely to come to one who is free from all attachments and able to exercise constant discrimination between the things that are true and those things that are false.

The use of the word "bodies" in the text is translated from the Sanskrit "śarīra"; it does not mean just the dense physical body, but includes all the subtle bodies. These subtle bodies extend beyond, and interpenetrate with, the physical body; when combined with the physical body, they form that part of man which is encompassed by the persona. This part is essentially finite; however, the reincarnating ego, which may be termed the spiritual individuality, is clearly of a less finite nature and includes the higher mental, buddhic and atmic planes of consciousness (which cannot really be described as "bodies" at all).[8]

The physical body may be thought of as a reflection or shadow of the etheric body, which is where the subatomic particles form the model or outline of the physical form. A disturbance in the etheric body is almost certain to be reflected on the physical plane and to lead to some physical or emotional disorder. Similarly, if the particles on the etheric plane are well ordered and vibrating as a harmonious whole, then the physical body to which they belong will be strong and fit and characterized by a healthy disposition.

This sūtra may be viewed from another perspective: namely, that the characteristics of the physical form are "chosen" by the yogi who meditates on the creative powers of the Divine. Knowledge of this power gives the yogi control over the natural elements from which the body is formed. In this way a body may actually be "created" for the accomplishment of a particular task.[9]

---

8. In yoga philosophy, the mind is normally divided into "higher" and "lower," as pertaining to normal brain-centered activity (the lower mind) and higher levels of consciousness/activity (the higher mind). The terms "buddhic" and atmic" are based on the Sanskrit words buddhi (the faculty of mental perception), and ātmā (spirit).

9. This notion of a "duplicate body" is a siddhi, or yogic power; it is described in the *Yoga Sūtras,* and is an entirely temporary phenomenon. Such occurrences have been witnessed by people seeing and conversing with a yogi, in full knowledge of his "actual" whereabouts in some distant place. It would be hard to prove the existence of such a duplicate body (which is totally unlike a clone), and it is not a central part of Śaivite philosophy. For this reason I have kept this as a footnote.

Sūtra 1.20

भूतसंधानभूतपृथक्त्वविश्वसंघट्टाः ।

bhūtasaṃdhāna-bhūtapṛthaktva-viśva-saṃghaṭṭāḥ

From contemplation on the five elements in nature (pañca-bhūtas) arises the capacity to analyze and separate them and to understand their function in the building of the universe.[10]

This aphorism is an amplification of the one before with regard to the creation of the universe. Śiva, as the Supreme Being, is accorded different attributes in different schools of philosophy. When identified with the Hindu Trinity, together with Brahma and Viṣṇu, Śiva is known as the Destroyer, or the cause of dissolution. However, in Śaivism, Śiva is the god of creation, preservation and destruction. The present object of attention is the first aspect.

Modern science has investigated the smallest components of matter, and particle physics can now reveal the nature of both atomic and subatomic particles. In the Indian tradition, the elements which combine to form matter are known as the pañca-

10. In *Metaphysics Zeta 17*, Aristotle writes: "Therefore what we seek is the cause, i.e., the form, by reason of which the matter is some definite thing; and this is the substance of the thing" *[1041b 1.8–9]*. He approaches the whole question of form, matter and the elements from a rather different perspective from the one under discussion. But in this passage, when Aristotle talks specifically about causation, the subject is not so far removed from the Kaśmiri text. *Complete Works*, ed. J. Barnes, Princeton, 1984.

bhūtas, i.e., the five elements or components of nature: earth, fire, water, air and ether. Western science is familiar with the first four, but only recently has any notice been taken of the etheric plane and the subatomic particles of which it is composed. Essentially, the five elements are the differentiated elements in Nature, which combine to form the particles from which all animate and inanimate objects in the manifested universe are made.[11]

The elements, which give rise to root substance, are secondary only to consciousness, in which lies the true origin of all manifestation. Therefore it can be understood why it is so important for the yogi to be able to analyze and separate the various elements, if he or she is to exercise the Divine Power of Creation. The essential nature of each element can be comprehended by the practice of saṃdhāna (meditation) in relation to the individual elements. The first four elements, in their outward form, are all recognizable to the senses, but the fifth is rather different.

Ether is not ordinarily perceptible, but may be likened to ākāśa, or space, which is both infinite and all-pervasive. There is nowhere ākāśa is *not,* and its subatomic particles are the finest imaginable in essence. Far from being inert, they are highly active and provide the astral form, or etheric double, from which gross particles and forms are derived. So subtle and pliable is its nature that it actually "records" every act and intention that arises in the mind of man. Such a concept may stretch the pow-

11. In the philosophy of yoga this type of knowledge is classified in accordance with the science of tattvas, or true principles, and while they are applicable in the context of this work, they are not described at all in the original text.

ers of imagination, but the existence of the ākāśic records has long been known, and they can be "read" by one who is sensitive and tuned to the astral light.

The pañca-bhūtas form the root substance of all matter[12] and ether, the fifth element, is the vehicle of sound and all vibration. This description may help in understanding the fluidity and pervasiveness of the etheric state, because sound can penetrate all types of matter. Sound is a vibration, which may or may not be audible, and as the frequency changes, so the characteristics of that vibration change. Light, like sound, may or may not be perceptible to the senses, and it has been said that the human body is made from frozen particles of light, the vibrations of which have slowed sufficiently to enable matter to form around them. Knowledge of the function of the elements can be seen, therefore, to be essential to the understanding of the universe and the creative powers in man.

12. This was a thorny problem for Aristotle and he expended much effort trying to resolve the question of form, substance and root matter. In *Physics 1*, chapter 2, he admits to the possibility of there being any number of elements, but his antecedents did not extend further back than the early Greek philosophers. Because there was no means to identify or describe anything beyond the three or four known elements, knowledge of *ether* lay outside of both science and philosophy for many centuries to come (although it was known to the medieval alchemists). Sir Isaac Newton's descriptions of ether do not conform to current theories, and a discrepancy still remains between the old and new science, and between the Eastern and the Western views on this point.

Sūtra 1.21

शुद्धविद्योदयाच्चक्रेशत्वसिद्धिः ।

śuddha-vidyodayāc-cakreśatva-siddhiḥ

On the dawning of pure, unmodified knowledge, mastery is gained over the Great Center, through which the Divine manifests in the phenomenal world.

Ordinary knowledge is obtained from one's own memory bank, from the experience of another person, or from present experience (i.e., in the form of empirical knowledge). This knowledge, whether it relates to facts or ideas, is by definition thought-based. The information or experience which gives rise to this knowledge is conceived, stored and retrieved by a process of thought, which then finds expression in words.

Pure, unmodified knowledge is altogether different.[13] Such knowledge is concerned with truth, or with the absolute, and is neither limited by personal experience nor dependent upon memory, thought or verbal expression. It has, as it were, an independent objective existence, and where an object is perceived by the senses, it is perceived by an individual from a particular viewpoint. Knowledge which is derived from that object is therefore filtered by subjective experience, and is limited to the angle of perception. For a given object to be perceived in its totality would require that it be seen from all sides at once and

13. viz. *Śiva Sūtras 3:18.*

to be perceived by all the senses, devoid of subjective experience and any preconception. Unmodified knowledge is not confined to objects; on the contrary, it is concerned with concepts, principles and ideas, and is capable of encompassing them from all angles, without prejudice and also without illusion.

The Great Center (mahābindu) is in some respects analogous to the waist of a traditional sand-filled timer. The analogy is purely descriptive, in that the realm of spirit and unmodified knowledge is not physically separate from the worlds of manifestation and ordinary knowledge. However, there has to be a point of entry from one realm to the other (or from one glass chamber to the other), even if that point is *meta*-physical, rather than physical.[14] It follows, therefore, that mastery over this point enables one to open wide the doorway between the spiritual and material worlds. The key to this door is unmodified knowledge; once in possession of it, everything is ultimately attainable, because individual consciousness is then united with the Divine Power of Śiva, in a state of true omniscience. Different words may be used, according to different traditions, but the meaning remains the same, whether the dedication is to Īśvara, Parabrahman, or simply the "God within."

14. viz. *Śiva Sūtras 1:16.*

Sūtra 1.22

महाह्रदानुसंधानान्मन्त्रवीर्यानुभवः ।

mahāhradānu-saṃdhānānmantra-vīryānubhavaḥ

Deep contemplation on that power which is the Will of the Divine (the Supreme Śakti) leads to an understanding of the creative force of sound (expressed in mantra).

This is a complex sūtra of deep significance, alluding to occult truths about the Divine Will, the hidden powers of sound, and the manifestation of the universe. The written word is unable to communicate the full mystery of Life and Creation, least of all in a language which evolved through concrete, rational thought (i.e., English). Para-śakti (the Supreme Śakti) is perhaps the key to understanding the link between the forces described, because it (she) embodies the whole principle of Divine Ideation and creativity. Mantra is an expression of this energy, which helps to unite the highest faculties in man with the spirit of Universal Consciousness.

The nature and properties of sound were first discussed in Sūtra 1.4. Divine Energy is a power that emanates from a point or center, and fills the whole universe. Might not this energy be the essence of life itself? If the source of this energy is recognized as being within the realm of consciousness, then it is possible for the yogi to gain mastery over it, by uniting his consciousness with that of the Divine.

Mantra, which is an invocation to the Spirit of Divine Consciousness, is a highly organized form of sound. Sound is the vehicle of expression projected through the mind, and the intent behind the sound determines the form of the sound produced. A mantra may in essence be an expression of adoration, an invocation to the unity, or a recognition of the divine origin of man. "Oṃ," the shortest and most widely used mantra, has the effect of aligning the centers which serve as vortices of energy, and these centers (cakras) lie principally on the midline of the body. The production of the sound "Oṃ" begins with the lungs full and the mouth open. It continues until the breath is spent, and the sound, as it were, passes through the top of the head, with the mouth almost closed. It is known as the praṇava [ॐ], and is made up of three sounds—A U M—which merge to form the one sacred syllable. Mantra can be extended into a whole system of chanting, and is practiced in different forms by monks, brahmins and yogis around the world, and has been for thousands of years.

Sound, in the ordinary sense, is an everyday part of life, but it tends only to occupy our consciousness when the sound is invasive and demanding of attention. The nature of sound being discussed in the present context, however, is of a rather special order. The production of such a sound (mantra) requires energy, which implies motion, and it results in a particular vibration, which, to the tuned faculties of the yogi, embodies the secret of manifestation.

Book Two

Śāktopāya: The Realization of Śakti

Sūtra 2.1

चित्तं मन्त्रः ।

cittaṃ mantraḥ

Mind-consciousness is a vibration, the nature of which is expressed in mantra.

Book Two is the shortest of the three books, and this sūtra is one of several aphorisms comprising just two words in the original Sanskrit. Citta, it has been said, is a principle, not an object, and I translate it here as "mind-consciousness." Citta emanates from the Divine Will, but it becomes veiled as it materializes in man, and whereas ātmā has the nature of pure consciousness, and is absolute, citta by contrast, is limited.[15] It is a derivative of ātmā, but in man, citta is no longer pure spirit. It has the potential to be reunited with ātmā, but conscious awareness of the individual self, which is a characteristic of all human beings, is not the same as union with the true Inner Self.

Mind is an interaction between spirit and matter, and although it may be biased towards one or the other at different times, it does not exist in isolation, and interaction between the two is inherent. Mind is best described as a reflection of consciousness, and as such, consciousness can only be perceived when the mind itself is still. Constant movement or modifications in the mind prevent it from accurately reflecting the true nature of consciousness. Mind is a vehicle of perception, and it requires training for it to perform its special task of becoming absorbed (or reabsorbed) in pure consciousness. Union of mind and consciousness is thus achieved through meditation and japa (the constant repetition of a mantra), allowing the spirit of consciousness to be perceived by the still mind.

Mantra is a combination of sounds, which if correctly used, serve as an invocation to the Divine. Sound is generated by motion, or energy, whereby particles vibrate in the ether of space. Mantra is a sequence of vibrations which has a particular power,

15. In other words, thoughts are objects, or things, and are *particular*, whereas ātmā is essentially *universal*. Citta is both a vehicle and a medium of communication (or expression), and can give rise to thoughts and modifications of the mind. It can also be directed towards ātmā in meditation, as well as through the use of mantra. Its attributes are therefore dependent upon use. Yoga, which is the state of union between citta and ātmā, pertains to different mind states from those used by Western philosophers and psychologists. It can be misleading to try to compare the two systems when the conceptual basis is different, and not just the language that is employed.

and that power is focused through citta. It has been explained how mind operates on the etheric plane, and although mind produces no audible sound, etheric particles are made to vibrate, and can be directed by the will over any distance. An invocation is made by generating audible sound, or by generating a thought wave, and both have the effect of helping to unite citta and ātmā. Mantra *and* citta function through the medium of space (ākāśa), and have the same characteristics of vibration.

The nature and power of sound were discussed in Book One, but the link between sound and thought needs further comment. Thought is a manifestation or creation of the mind (citta), and citta is derived from the absolute consciousness of the Divine (ātmā). In respect of the origin of thought, if its outward expression is a vibration (or more particularly a mantra), then it has the potential to link the ordinary self, as mind-consciousness, with the Inner Self, or ātmā, through the medium of the ether. Ether, it has been said, is a "fluid" which fills all space (ākāśa), and it even extends to the cavities of the Earth and of the human body. Will, or consciousness, when expressed through mantra, therefore is a potent means of communication through the medium of space.

Sūtra 2.2

प्रयत्नः साधकः ।

prayatnaḥ sādhakaḥ

Persevering effort is the means of achieving knowledge of the relationship between citta and mantra.

Knowledge of the relationship between citta and mantra must go beyond intellectual understanding, and it has to be of an intuitive nature. Whilst it is possible to acquire knowledge in a flash of intuition, it is more normally gained by sustained effort and perseverance. Real understanding does not arise, therefore, without a foundation of knowledge, acquired by study and experience over time. Yoga and meditation can be practiced over long periods before a metaphysical understanding of the universe and knowledge of the Inner Self are acquired. Inspiration may come in flashes, but the groundwork must be laid in order for the conditions to be right, and persevering effort must be expended if the sādhaka is to be enlightened by the use of mantra.[16]

---

16. viz. *Śiva Sūtras 1:12.*

Sūtra 2.3

विद्याशरीरसत्ता मन्त्ररहस्यम् ।

vidyā-śarīra-sattā mantra-rahasyam

Knowledge of the One Reality is contained within the vehicle of consciousness, and may be revealed through the secrets of mantra.

The issue of universal and pre-existing knowledge is raised in this sūtra. When intellect and creativity are functioning in their highest form, one needs to consider the source of understanding or inspiration which may arise. Material and empirical knowledge exist in the field of the known, and arise from memory and experience. However, it is understood that the mind principle (citta) is tuned to the vibrations of the Inner Self (ātmā) when functioning at the highest level, and this experience is not the same as the first.[17]

It is said that the universe is a manifestation of the Divine Will (i.e., an expression of the Will of Śiva). Knowledge which is considered new to man has to originate somewhere. If that

17. The English language can *describe* different categories of knowledge, but the word "knowledge" remains the same. In Sanskrit there are different words for the different types of knowledge, and in this sūtra "vidyā" appears, not "jñāna." "Avidyā" is the word used for ignorance, and "vidyā" is its opposite, meaning ordinary or scientific knowledge. "Jñāna" is a different type of knowledge [viz. *Śiva Sūtras 1:2,4,8,17*] but it must be conceded that usage and context do have a bearing. "Vidyā" here pertains to higher knowledge, and "jñāna" refers to ordinary knowledge. This confusion is difficult to avoid, and the sense of the sūtras in question is quite wrong if the words are applied the other way around.

knowledge is prior, i.e., pre-existent in the universal consciousness, then individual consciousness is tapping that source.[18]

Knowledge of the One Reality is said to be contained within the vehicle of consciousness, and the practice of mantra enables that knowledge to be revealed. The major religions of the world agree that man is divine in origin, but the ways of interpreting that knowledge are legion. If man *is* essentially divine, then the essence of that divinity must be within the higher consciousness. Ways need to be found of realizing that divinity, and in that mantra has the capacity to form a bridge between the lower and higher manas (mind), then it may be imagined how the secrets of mantra can help reveal the secrets of the One Reality.

While still discussing mantra, it would be wrong to assume that its secrets will be given up to anybody uttering the appropriate sounds. The universe functions according to laws which are immutable; all men and all life are subject to these laws, and they cannot be overridden. In a sense, the chanting of mantra is both an art and a science, which few are qualified to teach (and even fewer able to perfect). The question of preconditions is relevant at this point; for example, if the heart is full of envy or hatred, or if the mind is preoccupied with matters of self-interest, it is unlikely that consciousness can be so tuned to the Inner Self as to be able to comprehend or recognize any such secrets. Mantra has a power which requires both discipline and respect as to its sanctity, and the study of mantra should be

18. Therefore, so-called discoveries may actually be rediscoveries of forgotten knowledge belonging to a previous age. But I concede that is a matter of conjecture by reason of the incapability of proving such an assertion.

approached with some deference, and a little caution, with regard to its potency. Mantra has one goal, although it can function in two ways: it can open up the channel of communication between ātmā and citta, and it can also help to steady the mind and direct it towards opening the channel (for which purpose it is most commonly used).

Sūtra 2.4

गर्भे चित्तविकासोऽविशिष्टविद्यास्वप्नः ।

garbhe citta-vikāso'viśiṣṭa-vidyā-svapnaḥ

Ordinary knowledge which unfolds within the limitations of the mind is dreamlike, and lacking in reality.

This sūtra describes the essential limitation of ordinary knowledge, which unfolds within the mind (as distinct from knowledge which is gained through the application of mantra). Consciousness is capable of expanding beyond the limitations of the mind, and it is not bound by the ordinary realms of thought. Ordinary waking consciousness is experienced through the senses, which in turn give rise to thought, but the student of yoga knows that this state of consciousness can be transcended by focusing the mind and piercing the veil of illusion.

Ordinary knowledge belongs to the reasoning mind, and however well the intellect may be developed, this knowledge is confined to the field of the known, within the manifested universe. In other words, it is in contrast to the subject of the previous sūtra. The unknown cannot be experienced by "the knower" if the mind which is perceiving is clouded by "false" images. Images appear before the mind, but the object of attention is ordinarily "the known," and the images that arise are not the essence of the object but its shadow or gross manifestation.

Sūtra 2.5

विद्यासमुत्थाने स्वाभाविके खेचरी
शिवावस्था ।

vidyā-samutthāne svābhāvike khecarī śivā-vasthā

That knowledge which is characterized by the absence of self leads, by correct application, to an understanding of the Ultimate Reality which exists in the void state, or Śiva.

Unlike ordinary knowledge, knowledge which is characterized by the absence of self is not limited. When the knower is able to perceive the known without subjectivity, attention is directed towards the object, or concept, simultaneously from all sides. It has been said that in the phenomenal world, or the world of shadows, objects (in reality) are not as they appear, on account of the division between the knower, the known and the state of knowing. This can be attributed to the power of illusion (māyā), and illusion is dispelled by the application of true knowledge towards the realization of the Ultimate Reality. True knowledge is both pure and absolute, it is unaffected by half-truth and subjectivity, and it pre-exists in the void state, known as Śiva, the Self-illumined. Within this void state, which is universally present, lies the infinite power of creativity from which all manifestation is derived.

Sūtra 2.6

गुरुरुपायः ।

gurur-upāyaḥ

A spiritual teacher may provide the means of enlightenment.

The question of gurus is raised here; this issue is at times controversial, and recent interest in Eastern philosophy has led to some Westerners traveling to India in search of a guru and some form of personal enlightenment. The great teachers of the world have themselves had their teachers;[19] nonetheless, spiritual transformation requires more than a passive acceptance of any particular teaching. The secrets of the spirit are hidden in the teachings of the Ancient Wisdom, and are revealed when the

---

19. An exception to this rule arises in the case of avatars. Avatars are no ordinary beings, but are incarnations of the Divine, who have no need to go through the normal stages of instruction and initiation, because they are enlightened from birth. Lord Kṛṣṇa and Lord Jesus are examples of avatars from earlier periods, and at the present time there are said to be avatars who have taken on the human vesture. These include Satya Sai Baba and the Holy Mother, Meera; the former has an aśram in south India, and the latter, who was born in India, lives in a small village in southern Germany. They both have countless devotees from all around the world.

aspirant is suitably prepared, which is normally after a period of sustained sacrifice and effort.

Emphasis is laid in classical Indian teaching on the need to find a guru; however, the pupil should not be compelled to go in search of a guru, or to live in an aśram. It is said that when the pupil is ready, the master will always be found. The essential issues are therefore spirituality and readiness, both of which are internal states, which have little to do with geographical location or physical proximity. The seeds have to be sown before the fruit will appear, and the mind must be inward-turned before the Inner Light is perceived or the teacher is recognized.

Once the pupil has found his or her master, a bond is then formed which is stronger than ordinary personal ties. The relationship has a basis in spirituality, and the unique quality of the bond is significant to both persons, although for different reasons. The pupil shows love and respect towards the master in deference to his wisdom, and in gratitude for effort expended on his behalf. The master, or guru, on the other hand, by agreeing to instruct the pupil, assumes a direct responsibility for the actions of the pupil (sādhaka), in whom he too places trust. Love, respect and trust are all characteristics of the relationship which exists between them; however, the karma which the pupil may then generate is shared by both master and pupil. The consequence of wrongful action by the sādhaka is therefore damaging and painful to the master, so it is something of special significance when the pupil is accepted by a guru.

It is necessary to "beware false gurus," and there is no shortage of volunteers to assume that particular mantle. It is said that it takes one spiritual being to recognize another, and a guru who is self-proclaimed may not be genuine. A process of mutual recognition is more likely to occur, whereby the master finds a pupil who is ready for instruction, and the pupil finds a master who can satisfy his or her spiritual aspirations. If the circumstances are right, therefore, it is possible for the guru to provide "the means of admission to the temple of Divine Wisdom." Such an entry may be gained by the acquisition of the secret knowledge of mantra, directly from the guru; in fact, it cannot be gained without a guru, according to ancient tradition.

Sūtra 2.7

मातृकाचक्रसंबोधः ।

mātṛkā-cakra-saṃbodhaḥ

Union of pupil and Master arises from knowledge of the hidden meaning of sound, and from an expansion of consciousness through mantra, which unites all the cakras of the body.

The relationship between guru and disciple, or master and pupil, is of a very different nature from that between an ordinary teacher and pupil. The bonds of karma have already been described, and the present sūtra concerns another aspect of that relationship. Students of classical Indian teachings will be familiar with the cakra system, in which various centers in the body act as vortices for the distribution of vital energy (prāṇa).

These cakras have a vital role to play in the maintenance of health and well-being, and a disturbance in any one of these centers, which serve to connect the gross physical body with the subtle etheric body, may give rise to dysfunction or disease.

These centers must be correctly balanced, and the subject of this sūtra is not so much the physical health of the sādhaka as the spiritual development, for which the master has assumed responsibility. The importance of mantra is underlined in the present sūtra, which alludes to the secret knowledge of sounds, deriving from the Sanskrit. The language of Sanskrit is not sacerdotal, and its construction and organization are quite scientific. Each character is a sound produced by a particular part of the verbal apparatus. For example, palatals, dentals and labials are all separately grouped, and because each different sound has a separate character, Sanskrit has more than double the number of vowels found in the Roman alphabet. This avoids ambiguity and inconsistencies, both of which abound in the English language (something well known to students for whom English is a foreign language).

Each sound has a metaphysical connection, and in broad terms the vowels are concerned with the Inner Creation, and the consonants, the Outer Creation. For example, "ha" [ह] is the letter of immortality, and the two dots of its abbreviated form [ः] (visarga) represent the Sun and the Moon. In another example, the initial letter "a" [अ] is said to represent the First Ray, which is manifest in the consciousness of the ego. The characters, in other words, are concerned with sound and concepts (unlike, for example, Mandarin, where the characters are pictorial representations).

The cakras are principally located on the midline of the body, and they connect points along the central axis, through which the "serpent fire" of kuṇḍalinī flows. The "serpent fire" flows up the spinal cord from the base of the spine to the brain, and this pathway is threefold, comprising iḍā and piṅgalā (which crisscross, serpent-like, to left and right) and suṣumnā, which flows straight up the center.[20] Iḍā is the channel for the negative, or feminine, force of creativity, and piṅgalā is the channel for the positive, masculine force, which finds expression as power and energy. Normally these forces do not pass further than the stem of the brain, and the crown cakra on the top of the head only opens with spiritual advancement, drawing energy up the central axis. The power of sound in mantra and the expansion of consciousness may now be seen to link together through the cakra system of the body, with the guru providing guidance and a degree of control.

20. viz. Caduceus, the Western symbol of medicine; see also *Śiva Sūtras 3:44*.

Sūtra 2.8

शरीरं हविः ।

śarīraṃ haviḥ

Everything is consumed in the supreme fire of consciousness.

After opening up appropriate cakras in the body, the pupil is ready to progress to a higher level of spiritual development, whereupon consciousness itself is transformed, and a deeper understanding of the mysteries of life arises. The vehicle of desire which binds the individual to the ordinary plane of existence can be finally consumed, with guidance from the guru, making the sādhaka safe from the ever present danger of falling backwards down the steep path, ascended by sustained, conscious effort. Desires can be suppressed or ignored, but there remains the possibility of the flame being rekindled, without the final destruction of the lower vehicle of consciousness (i.e., ordinary thoughts, emotions and desires, which belong to the physical human form).

This destruction is of the limitations of consciousness, and is actually a transformation that results in the ability to control desires. This process is described in different ways by different teachers, and while traditional interpretations tend to be in accord with tantric philosophy (the language of which is sometimes quite powerful), it is really an inner change that takes place, which is both silent and invisible. Desires have the power to bind the individual, thus blocking all hope of transformation, and mastery of even the memory of desires is needed in order for the sādhaka to attain the higher levels of consciousness.

Sūtra 2.9

ज्ञानमन्नम् ।

jñānam-annam

Freedom arises from the destruction of ordinary knowledge.

The mind is a wonderful instrument which is capable of great subtlety of expression. It can also be an instrument of power and limitless capacity, but to perform in this way it must be tuned to the Will of the Divine; the mind must also be like an empty vessel, and not filled with accumulated "debris." Everyday thoughts and actions are often geared toward the acquisition of knowledge and wealth. It is maintained that knowledge of Reality *can* be attained while living in the material word, but it is important that the mind is unhindered by obstacles, which include all forms of attachment.[21] No vessel is of use if its capacity is already taken up; similarly, the mind cannot provide a

21. The obstacles which inhibit the power of mantra are listed in Book One of the *Yoga Sūtras.* In addition to the symptoms of a distracted mind, such as sorrow, despair, nervousness and difficult breathing, the means to overcome these obstacles are given. When the mind is freed and the obstacles or kleśas have been overcome, the result is "perfect mastery extending from the finest atom to the greatest infinity," according to Patanjali [viz. *Yoga Sūtras 1:31–41*].

channel of communication between the ātmā and ordinary consciousness if that channel is blocked with debris. Communication is achieved when consciousness is no longer dominated by the faculties of sensory perception, because ordinarily the individuality identifies with, and is then bound to, the source of such impressions.

Ordinary knowledge is easily assimilated when assigned to its proper place; the mind should be detached from ordinary knowledge and from sensory input, since neither should dominate the mental faculties or weaken control over the application and content of the mind. Thought otherwise sustains attachment, memory and desire, which are obstacles on the path of enlightenment.

Sūtra 2.10

विद्यासंहारे तदुत्थस्वप्नदर्शनम् ।

vidyā-saṃhāre taduttha-svapna-darśanam

Realization of the dreamlike nature of the phenomenal world arises from the destruction of ordinary knowledge.

When this destruction has taken place, with regard to the causes of bondage and suffering, awareness of the true nature of Reality arises, together with a perception of the lack of reality in the dreamlike, phenomenal worlds. In this sūtra, the subject of Self-realization is raised once again. Every journey must have its purpose, and the purpose of this journey through the whole field of emotions, sense impressions and the different states of consciousness is the attainment of Self-realization. This is the goal for which so much effort and many lifetimes are expended. Unless each individual comes to know his or her own true identity as an "outpost" of Divine Consciousness, then the whole process of birth, growth and decay is without real meaning.

The essence of Book Two is such that realization of the true nature of Self can come about only when the dreamlike nature of the phenomenal world is perceived, and not mistaken for the One Reality. With this perception comes the destruction of illusion and ordinary knowledge, which otherwise enslave the mind. Through Self-realization, consciousness is transmuted from identity with the senses, and from separateness, to that state of awareness in which the personal self ceases to exist (for its own sake). When the mind is fully tuned to the spirit, then a channel of communication opens up with the consciousness of the Divine (Śiva), which is within. Mantra has the power to facilitate this process of transformation.

BOOK THREE

Āṇavopāya: The Realization of the Atmic Energy of the Supreme Being

Sūtra 3.1

आत्मा चित्तम् ।

ātmā cittam

Ātmā and citta are essentially the same, mind being an aspect of consciousness.[22]

Consciousness pre-exists all forms of manifestation, and in its ultimate state it is the creative force from which everything in the universe springs. It cannot easily be defined, because all that can truly be said about it is the extent to which it is reflected in the mind. A definition is normally based on the properties and characteristics of a thing, which may be an

22. See also the first sūtras of Books One and Two of the *Śiva Sūtras*.

object or idea, but such descriptive terms do not reveal the true essence of a thing, and consciousness is clearly no exception.

A mind that is pure, unselfish and attuned to the Universal Consciousness is of an entirely different nature from that of an ordinary individual. The mind can be like a finely tuned instrument, and as such it has an infinite capacity for knowledge and for wisdom. Ordinary knowledge is the product of the intellect and experience, and it can limit the creative power of the mind more readily than set it free; but when that knowledge springs from the heart, it has a different quality. If the head and the heart work together, a power can be generated which unites the mind with the spirit of Universal Consciousness.

The capacity of the mind is without limitation if the obstacles (kleśas) are removed, and if the mind is free to function as "a transparent jewel."[23] The light of true knowledge is radiant, and serves to unite both mind and consciousness; this radiance has the power to transcend all ordinary knowledge, and emanates from the Inner Light, or luminosity.

Consciousness may be said to exist at all levels, from the most mundane to the most spiritual, but this does not suppose that consciousness is personal or fragmented. It exists in its Divine Purity irrespective of any human perception. What does vary is the capacity of each monad or "outpost" of consciousness to become an evolved human form and mirror the Universal Consciousness. Each human being is empowered

---

23. viz. the *Yoga Sūtras* of Patanjali, Book Two for a description of the obstacles and the method to overcome them; reference to mind as "a transparent jewel" can be found in *Yoga Sūtras 1:41*.

with certain choices, and the manner in which such power is expressed, and the wisdom of choices made, will vary in every individual. The power to reason, the capacity to learn and the will to learn are further variables of the mind state, and a balance is needed between the capacity to learn and the will to learn.

Unity of mind and consciousness is a potentiality, and a reality, depending on the actual state of mind and consciousness. For the yogi who has achieved the state of union it is a reality, but for others it is a potentiality. Even when this union is lacking, though, the reality is ever present and the state of union is the ultimate state to which all strive, whether it is actually apprehended or not. The *Śiva Sūtras* do not describe the pathway to the state of union, rather they reveal the nature of mind and consciousness, which itself is an object of meditation. The mind that is inward-turned is thus able to acquire Self-knowledge and realize full Self-consciousness.[24]

24. Self-consciousness being awareness of the identity of the Self with the Supreme Being, not knowledge of the ordinary separate self.

Sūtra 3.2

ज्ञानं बन्धः ।

jñānaṃ bandhaḥ

Ordinary knowledge is a cause of bondage, mind being the creator of illusion.

There can be no awareness of the union of mind and consciousness if the citta (thinking principle) is outward-turned, because the mind cannot be both inward-turned and outward-turned at the same time. Similarly, the pathway of meditation and self-knowledge cannot be the same as the pathway to material learning. The mind may be highly developed, but so preoccupied with knowledge and experience that it is not capable of reflection; "empty space" within the mind, so to speak, is needed for the development of intuitive knowledge.

There need be no renunciation of learning, because ordinary knowledge is an essential part of living. This sūtra underlines the point that learning for its own sake will not bear fruit, in terms of spiritual development, because the acquisition of ordinary knowledge hinders the turning inward of consciousness and the realization of the ātmā. The yogi who has developed the power of intuition and who has experienced Self-knowledge does not necessarily function in a state of continuous enlightenment. Knowledge can be directed with great effect towards the material plane, but because there is no attachment or illusion, the mind is free to switch at will from the everyday affairs of life towards inner contemplation.

Sūtra 3.3

कलादीनां तत्त्वानामविवेको माया ।

kalādīnāṃ tattvānām-aviveko māyā

The great illusion arises from the inability to discriminate between the ordinary perception of objects and the understanding of their true inner qualities.

References to illusion are often found in the philosophy of yoga, and this Great Illusion is none other than life itself, as lived on the material plane. The reasoning mind is apt to describe the world of the senses as *reality,* and the non-physical world as *illusion.* This assumption is false, and one who seeks the inner meaning of life will know that all life is made up of the different aspects of the One Reality.

Wisdom and discrimination go hand in hand, and the seeker of wisdom learns to discriminate between the true and the false, the just and the unjust, the real and the illusory. Objects (i.e., anything on the material plane) are normally judged by their appearance, and not by their true characteristics, because the essence of a thing is not visible to the human eye. Every object has its own particular properties (guṇas), it is said, which may be dominated by stability, motion or equilibrium.[25] A stone, for example, may appear totally inert, but that inertia is an illusion, because all forms of matter vibrate, and even the stone has its

25. The three guṇas are known as tamas, rajas and sattva (which I have translated as stability, motion and equilibrium).

own particular vibration. The stone has various characteristics which determine its outward form, but they do not take away from its unseen properties. For example, in the case of a precious or semi-precious stone, it may have dynamic powers which stem from the inner characteristics of the stone. These are sometimes used in healing and also for religious purposes.

In the *Yoga Sūtras,*[26] Patanjali writes about the coming together of the Seer and the Seen, and gives ignorance as being the cause of bondage between the two. Illusion arises out of ignorance about the true nature of form and about the world of manifestation. That which passes for reality is only a shadow projected onto the wall of objectivity. Perception of truth is only as complete as the instrument which perceives it; therefore, if the mind is impure, the images which are projected by that mind will be partial, impure and unable to reflect the whole truth. Concrete, irrefutable proof is hard to establish in order to convince the skeptic of things which cannot be seen. The inability to discriminate between the ordinary perception of objects and the incapacity to understand their real nature *perpetuate* illusion, and are the products of ignorance, or literally "not-knowing." Meditation on the true nature of Reality and the practice of discrimination provide the means to unravel the mysteries of life and the relationship between the Seer and the Seen.

---

26. viz. *Yoga Sūtras 2:20–24.*

Sūtra 3.4

शरीरे संहारः कलानाम् ।

śarīre saṃhāraḥ kalānām

When consciousness transcends the vehicles of bondage, the various principles through which they functioned become reabsorbed into the integrated state (having no further use).

Each aspect of consciousness has an appropriate vehicle or mode of expression. When the mind is not fully developed, it is incapable of expressing the highest aspects of consciousness, but as the capacity grows to respond to the finer vibrations, then the vehicles which pertain to the lower states of consciousness fall away.

The causes of bondage are overcome one by one, and as mastery is gained over the senses, the emotions and the lower mental states, so the capacity to respond to these vibrations dies. Vibrations from the lower planes will have no hold over the yogi, having previously gained mastery of the senses and control over the lower self. The senses and the emotions do not cease to exist, they simply cease to dominate or produce impressions which hold the mind. Those mental states which attach to the lower mind will fade, and as the vehicles of expression lose their power to respond, so the mind will gradually become tuned to a higher rate of vibration.

Realization of the One Reality is the goal, whereby the mind becomes reabsorbed into the integrated state of wholeness (pure spirit) from which it first evolved and to which it will eventually return in full Self-consciousness. Just as a child will discard the objects which surrounded it in childhood, so the spirit of consciousness will grow, and the objects which at one time preoccupied the mind will be discarded. So, something which evokes a strong response at an early phase of spiritual evolution does nothing to disturb the consciousness when perfect equilibrium has been attained. Unrestrained emotion that at first produces a whole wave of response eventually becomes no more than a ripple; it fades of its own accord as progress is made along the spiritual path.

Sūtra 3.5

नाडीसंहार-भूतजय-भूतकैवल्य-
भूतपृथक्त्वानि ।

**nāḍīsaṃhāra-bhūtajaya-bhūtakaivalya-
bhūtapṛthaktvāni**

Mastery over the pañca-bhūtas and the capacity to isolate and differentiate one from another is attained by purification of the nāḍīs (which channel the subtle energies of the body).

The nāḍīs are minute channels which enable the circulation of vital energy around the body; by interrupting the flow, consciousness can be directed towards the component elements (bhūtas) in their separated form. This capacity arises from the purification of the nāḍīs, and results in an understanding of the true nature of matter.

The five-element theory of the pañca-bhūtas is an important part of oriental philosophy, and is not confined to one school or system. Variations on the theory have spread outward from India and China over several thousand years. Aspects of it have been incorporated into religion, astrology, and some branches of medicine.[27]

The space immediately surrounding the human body is closely linked to the physical body and holds its etheric counterpart. This counterpart belongs to the subtle plane of existence, and although it is without capacity for ordinary sensory perception, it is able to receive and communicate impressions, which ordinarily leave no trace in the mind. However, as the mind becomes attuned to these impressions, it will respond to impressions received through the subtle body as well as to impressions received through the mind and the physical senses. If the yogi is to expand his consciousness and transcend the limitations of the physical body, he must understand the nature and composition of the elements from which it is made. Mastery over the elements has nothing to do with the personal self, but has to do with accomplishment of the goal of spiritual union with Śiva, achieved through the purification of the nāḍīs.

---

27. viz. *Śiva Sūtras 1:20*. Medicine, astrology and religion are separate areas of study in the modern world, but that has not always been the case. For example, tantric Tibetan medicine brings all three together and even now requires that student doctors be thoroughly familiar with ancient Buddhist texts and the sciences of both medicine and astrology.

Sūtra 3.6

मोहावरणात् सिद्धिः ।

mohāvaraṇāt siddhiḥ

The accomplishment of siddhis may not remove the causes of delusion which hinder the perception of reality.

The accomplishment of siddhis has often attracted interest and curiosity, although the siddhis are largely unknown, especially in the West. The siddhis are a type of psychic phenomena which are quite specific in nature, and result from various stages of development. Many of them are described by Patanjali in Book Three of the *Yoga Sūtras;* however, a warning is given that they should not be pursued as objects in their own right.

Siddhis are accomplishments that naturally occur in the course of progress along the path of yoga. This path is one of spiritual development, and it must not be thought that the ability to employ superphysical powers is a measure of spirituality. Sometimes young children have the capacity to perform siddhis spontaneously, before any spiritual training is undertaken. Conversely, a disciple may have great wisdom and compassion without having acquired any siddhis. They are most likely to evolve over a period of time, during which the whole process of spiritual development will unfold.

Delusion, therefore, cannot be removed simply by the accomplishment of siddhis. Perception of Reality is hindered by many things, but the greatest obstacle comes from the mind itself. The mind is sometimes like an untamed animal, and it cannot be brought to heel without patient effort and endurance. When the mind is suitably trained, it offers no hindrance to the perception of Reality. Delusion is the prime cause of ignorance, and when this cause has been removed, the light of truth is free to shine and illumine the heart and mind.[28]

Sūtra 3.7

मोहजयादनन्ताभोगात् सहजविद्याजयः ।

mohajayād-anantābhogāt sahaja-vidyā-jayaḥ

From the complete ending of ignorance and delusion arises that knowledge which is infinite, pertaining to the nature of universal manifestation.

This sūtra requires little commentary, as its meaning is relatively clear. The hindrance imposed on the mind by ignorance and delusion has been described, and the knowledge which dispels this is *pure* knowledge, which in turn leads to an understanding of the nature of the universe. This is distinct from knowledge which is mundane and limiting on the mind. Pure knowledge is about beauty, truth and ātmā, and may ultimately reveal the secrets of the universe, which include the *cause* of manifestation. The universe functions according to law, and

28. viz. *Yoga Sūtras 2:1–11.*

from a complete understanding of this law arises mastery over the component elements in nature. Such knowledge is without limitation, and may lead to the acquisition of superphysical powers (siddhis).

Sūtra 3.8

जाग्रद्द्वितीयकरः ।

jāgrad-dvitīya-karaḥ

The waking state of consciousness is likened to a secondary effulgence of the Supreme Light of the Divine.

The effulgence, or Primary Ray, of the Supreme Light of the Divine is the ineffable Light of Divine Consciousness. When the Light finds expression in manifestation, the One becomes many, and the sparks which belong to the One Flame differentiate into so many monads (the monad being the spiritual entity which lies within the human form). The Primary Ray is without limitation, and the Secondary Ray is not fundamentally different, but is channeled into differentiated mind-consciousness, expressed in the wakeful state of jāgrat. Only the yogi who perceives the unity throughout Nature is wholly aware of this link with the Divine. This link is a reality, not an illusion, but cannot ordinarily be perceived for lack of awareness of the Truth. The Primary Effulgence will never penetrate the darkness of a mind that is unillumined; lack of awareness, on the other hand, cannot dim the Supreme Light of the Divine, because the Light always shines, even when unperceived.

The waking state is the ordinary state of consciousness perceived by the mind. More exalted states of consciousness may be experienced by the few who tread the path of spirituality, but every living being experiences ordinary waking consciousness (jāgrat) in some degree of awareness. If that ordinary state is an aspect of the Divine Consciousness, or Secondary Ray, then it is possible to identify the spark, or monad, and discover the essential spiritual nature of man. It is easy to imagine that an exalted state of enlightenment is spiritual in nature, but it is much harder to perceive the inherent spirituality of all existence, in relation to everyday waking consciousness.

It may be said that the Divine Will, or Consciousness (in its true purity), sustains all creation, and it is the vibration and density of matter which determine gross or subtle forms in manifestation. The Light of the Divine is referred to many times in the literature of the world's religions, and that light vibrates in its purity at an extremely high frequency, and has limitless power and energy. The degree of "condensation," or stepping down, determines the density of form, whereby the essence of matter, including the Earth itself, assumes physical form, as it reduces its speed of velocity. The Divine Light is an emanation from the One Supreme Consciousness. It can manifest therefore in countless different ways, but the further it descends into matter, the greater the obscuration.

Sūtra 3.9

नर्तक आत्मा ।

nartaka ātmā

One who has realized his spiritual nature is like a dancer, dancing to the rhythm of the universe.

The analogy of life and dance can be found in many cultural traditions, and dance, like music, has no meaning without rhythm. If the rhythm which sustains the dance is the rhythm of the universe, then that dance is truly sacred. The question which arises is how to perceive the rhythm of the universe. There is no answer to that question, beyond the indication that, as with all mysteries, the answer may lie within the depths of the human soul or the inner recesses of the heart. It is also worth remembering that one need not travel to the four corners of the Earth in order to find a mystery which is hidden within one's own Inner Self.

If the mind and emotions are preoccupied with sensory objects and personal relationships in the waking state of jāgrat, there is neither energy nor space (psychologically) to devote to the effort needed for the spiritual quest. However, when the consciousness of the individual is raised to a level of spiritual perception, then it is fitting to talk of "a dancer as dancing to the rhythm of the universe."

"The Dance of Śiva," or taṇḍava, is famous, and is depicted by Naṭarāja, the cosmic dancer. In one right hand (he is allegorically given two pairs of arms) he holds the cosmic drum of creation, which is a symbol of creation, and produces the primordial sound (śabda). This is the sound expressed through mantra, which provides the vehicle of expression for the creative power of sound. In one left hand is held a ball of flame, which is the symbol of destruction, transmutation, and, ultimately, also of regeneration. An outer circle of fire is normally described around the perimeter of the icon, and Naṭarāja is seen standing on an evil spirit, which symbolizes the conquest of good over evil. There are variations to this imagery, and just as there are many names for Śiva, so there are many different dances.

Another image frequently encountered in Śaivism is that of the Śivaliṅgam, which is known as "an auspicious symbol." It may assume different forms, most commonly that of a phallus and yoni. The attention of the reader may be drawn to the fact that liṅga are produced phenomenally by some yogis, when such objects assume a special importance.

Sūtra 3.10

रङ्गोऽन्तरात्मा ।

raṅgo'ntarātmā

The arena is a manifestation of the indwelling consciousness (or Śiva).

Sutras 9, 10 and 11 may be grouped together because they develop a single theme. A stage or arena is needed where the dancer can perform, and the dance, arena and audience may all be identified by analogy: the dancer is the individuality, or monad; the arena is the physical universe, or phenomenal world; and the audience comprises the sense organs, described in the next sūtra.

The unspoken question arising from this sūtra is "What is the true nature of the phenomenal world?" The *noumenal* world is best described as the plane of causes, from where root matter originates; by contrast, the *phenomenal* world is the world of effects, where root matter condenses to the point of materialization and assumes solid form and objectivity. This may be perceived as a definition of the entire physical world in which we live. All matter has life, and all matter vibrates, and that rate of vibration is infinitely variable. This rate determines the nature of form, which slowly ascends through the cycles of evolution until pure white light is reached, and matter returns to "that from which it came" (or the Essence).

"That from which it came" is really nameless, because it is

pure spirit, or the Indwelling Consciousness. Objects and people are named, but the act of naming limits *and* defines. To call a tree a tree means that in the mind of the perceiver preconceptions can arise. These refer to the characteristics of any tree, as well as to the characteristics of the tree which is beheld. The essence of "tree" is not normally perceived, because the eye and the mind identify the object with the aid of memory, without the means of "total perception."

The perceiver, the process of perceiving and the perceived itself are all essentially one. Each may appear to have attributes and characteristics, but these are mere illusion, because all three are part of the One Indwelling and Universal Consciousness. It is the clouding of the mind which prevents understanding; thought and memory interfere and set up a complex chain, whereby the object of perception becomes subject to intrinsic change, by interaction with the perceiver.

Such activity creates a backdrop against which the dance of the universe is performed. It is ceaseless, just as the workings of the mind are ceaseless in ordinary waking consciousness; the whole physical universe is essentially a manifestation of the Divine Will of Śiva, and without that expression of Will, all matter would totally disintegrate.

Sūtra 3.11

प्रेक्षकाणीन्द्रियाणि ।

prekṣakāṇīndriyāṇi

The sense organs are the spectators in the arena of life.

The sense organs are the "eyes and ears" of the Indwelling Consciousness, inhabiting the vehicle of the human body, and in the arena of life impressions are received by means of the physical senses. Their functioning is often imperfect, but they nonetheless provide the ordinary vehicle of communication between one individual and another. There is little purpose in the dancer "dancing to the rhythm of the universe" if there is nobody to witness the dance, or if there is no communication between one being and another in the ceaseless motion of life. No performance is complete without spectators, and any performer can attest to the importance of the collective energy of an audience, the nature of which can directly affect a performance. Hence, by analogy, the importance of the role of the sense organs.

The sense organs are capable of functioning at different levels, and in ordinary waking consciousness they provide the mind with impressions of places and people, aided by the powers of memory and imagination. Each of the senses is capable of refinement, and may be developed to a state in which the senses are transmuted to serve the needs of the Indwelling Consciousness, by responding at the subtle level.

On the journey of the soul to enlightenment, the senses serve a most important function, enabling the perception of all manner of experiences, whilst facilitating communication with others. As the sādhaka begins to approach the goal at the end of the journey, the twin processes of purification and transmutation take place. The senses, which to this point have filled the lower mind with impressions at a physical level, and dominated consciousness in the waking state (jāgrat), now become vehicles of subtle communication. The analogy of the stage and the arena of life is something of a recurring theme in literature, and was immortalized by Shakespeare:

> All the world's a stage,
> And all the men and women merely players;
> They have their exits and their entrances;
> And one man in his time plays many parts,
> His acts being seven ages.
>
> (*As You Like It,* act 2, scene 7)

Too often this quote is taken in its literal sense, which masks an inner meaning in relation to the cycle of life and death, or the wheel of birth and rebirth, whereby experience is gained in various lives through the temporary vehicles of the sense organs.

Sūtra 3.12

धीवशात्सत्त्वसिद्धिः ।

dhīvaśāt-sattva-siddhiḥ

Perfect equilibrium arises from mastery of intuitive perception.

The faculty of intuitive perception provides an alternative means of understanding to that which derives from memory and the senses. Logic and reasoning are tools of the intellect, and may develop to a point of perfection, but not everything in the universe can be understood by these means. The laws of Nature, for example, may only be observed through their outward manifestation in the passing of the seasons. Nature too has a soul, and *her* innermost workings can be understood through the higher faculties of perception.

Intuitive perception is the complement to sensory perception, and just as the physical senses can be developed, so too can the faculty of intuition. It is sometimes said that women are more naturally intuitive than men, on account of their closer contact with Nature. This may or may not be true, and does not alter the fact that men and women are *both* capable of developing intuition, by laying aside rational judgment and learning to perceive things as they really are, not as they outwardly appear. The ability to acquire this faculty is more dependent on being attuned to the Inner Self than on the development of special skills. A life which is led with self-discipline and restraint, in accordance with the yogic tradition, is likely to lead to harmony and equilibrium in relationships with all fellow beings, and also with Nature, unless there is some disturbance.

It is a logical extension of this idea to consider *mastery* of intuitive perception and the attainment of perfect equilibrium in both one's inner and outer life. The latter is only an extension of the former, and in order to develop the state of sattva, or balance between the opposing forces of inertia and activity, attention has to be paid to the inner life. This is in order to counter the overriding preoccupation with the outer life, which characterizes most people's daily lives. Mastery and perfection are concepts that *are* attainable, but not by ordinary means, and it is not possible for the mind to be both inward-turned and outward-turned at the same time. Spiritual goals do not preclude material goals, but material preoccupation makes the attainment of spiritual goals all but impossible.

Sūtra 3.13

सिद्धः स्वतन्त्रभावः ।

siddhaḥ svatantra-bhāvaḥ

From control over the power of intuitive perception arises independence of being, or freedom from the ordinary limitations of consciousness.

The key words in this translation are "freedom" and "independence." True freedom is a state of spirituality in which there is independence of being, which follows a transformation of consciousness whereby the ordinary limitations of mind and body offer no hindrance. One term is therefore implicit in the other, insomuch as independence of spirit gives rise to true freedom, and true freedom gives rise to spiritual independence. Many lives are expended in defense of so-called freedom, and whole nations aspire to self-determination and independence, while the true nature of freedom is misconceived. If these terms are misused in everyday language, it should not prevent their usage in the present context.

The question arises as to how this freedom can be achieved. The answer is to be found in the previous sūtra. What has been said about intuitive perception need not be repeated, but it *is* the acquisition of this faculty which gives rise to both freedom of spirit and independence of being. The path towards intuitive perception is internal, not external, and has to do with the state of mind and consciousness, and not the social environment.

Sūtra 3.14

यथा तत्र तथान्यत्र ।

yathā tatra tathānyatra

This freedom may be exercised by the yogi in any place or circumstance (i.e., outside the physical body).

Once the yogi has attained the state of freedom described in the previous sūtra, limitations connected to place or circumstance no longer present a problem. The siddhi may be employed whereby the physical body is quiescent, and the spirit entity occupies and animates another physical body. This other body may have been vacated by the physical death of the occupant, by the occupant being in a state of unconsciousness, or by conscious cooperation between two living beings. This phenomenon is not unknown in the East, and can increase the effective capacity of the yogi to perform special tasks.

The ordinary physical body can be a hindrance, in that it has need of food, rest and shelter and is unable to operate at a distance without recourse to travel. The superphysical body is not hindered in this way, and is essentially free to travel and make contact with other beings on less physical planes of existence. Thoughts and emotions can be projected by the will without any special power; when the yogi has gained freedom from the ordinary limitations of consciousness, he is able to operate through a physical vehicle at any distance, by the controlled application of the will. This power is known as svatantra śakti, or āveśa; the mechanics of it may seem mysterious, but in essence, all that the yogi does is accomplished by the understanding and application of predetermined laws of Nature (whether or not they are comprehended by others).[29]

Superphysical feats, we know, are not necessarily tokens of spirituality, but may nonetheless be exercised for spiritual ends. There are accounts in Eastern literature about leaving and returning to the physical body, and living over an extended period of time in the physical body, even for hundreds of years. Inhabiting successive bodies, mastering the processes of decay and achieving great feats of endurance are other types of siddhis, accomplished by understanding and employing the secret laws of Nature. There remain tasks which cannot easily be performed *without* a physical body, and if there is mastery of the physical body through self-discipline (without recourse to siddhis), the body may still be a very effective vehicle.

---

29. A good description of āveśa may be found in *H. P. Blavastky—Tibet and Tulku,* by Geoffrey Barborka (viz. chapter 15), Theosophical Publishing House, Adyar, India, 1966.

Sūtra 3.15

बीजावधानम् ।

bījāvadhānam

The attention of the yogi is focused on the source of the universe (within the mind).

Manifestation is an objective realization of the Universal Consciousness; the yogi therefore directs his attention towards the pursuit of the origin and nature of the universe. Knowledge of these can be found within the recesses of the yogi's inner consciousness, and can be reflected upon by the mind, when inward-turned. This understanding stems from the mastery of intuitive perception, the mind of the yogi being inward-turned to allow the Light of Consciousness to illumine the mind. This is no intellectual exercise, but the result of "soul-learning," inspired by a love of humanity and radiating from the heart center within. This center is like the Sun, which continually shines to illumine the surrounding universe, and it is a source of limitless power and energy.

Sūtra 3.16

आसनस्थः सुखं ह्रदे निमज्जति ।

āsanasthaḥ sukhaṃ hrade nimajjati

He whose consciousness is centered on the supreme ātmā is plunged without effort into the ocean of bliss and immortality.

The language of this sūtra is descriptive in relation to the spiritual effect of uniting the consciousness of the yogi with the Supreme Being (Śiva). The sādhaka learns that the fruits of his or her endeavors may be in this life, not the next, as the yogi plunges into "the ocean of bliss and immortality." This *may* occur suddenly and "without effort," and although effort is normally expended along the way, a point of contact is made when the outer self becomes wholly submersed in the inner self, when bliss, enlightenment and immortality will result (as surely as night follows day).

Sometimes moments of union in everyday life are like flashes of inspiration, arriving when least expected, but the experience related here is different, by reason of its sublimity and irreversible nature. Never again will consciousness be bound by illusion, and the spirit will no longer be immersed in saṃsāra. Spiritual transformation is beyond the confines of time. Even the death of the physical body cannot reverse the changes which have occurred, and which will undoubtedly be manifest in future incarnations.

Sūtra 3.17

स्वमात्रानिर्माणमापादयति ।

svamātrā-nirmāṇam-āpādayati

The yogi thus attains the power of creation, in accordance with the measure of consciousness.

The power of creation is assigned to the Supreme Deity in the doctrine of most religions. In the yoga tradition there is a difference of understanding, in that if the consciousness of the yogi totally identifies with the Supreme Deity, then the power of creation is also attained by the yogi, as a result of an expression of Will. Consciousness is capable of infinite expansion, and when the Will is properly channeled, its creative powers transcend all limitation.

The term "creation" is capable of differing interpretations. It can apply to objects on the physical plane, but it can also apply to thoughts and activities, because without the creative power of thought, nothing would appear in objective manifestation, and no idea would ever take form. The individual capacity for creativity, in its literal sense, is determined by the state of consciousness and degree of attunement to the Divine Will, and this attunement serves as a measure, or gauge, of the state of the spiritual union achieved.

Sūtra 3.18

विद्याऽविनाशे जन्मविनाशः ।

vidyā'vināśe janma-vināśaḥ

Pure, unmodified knowledge, which causes the destruction of ordinary knowledge, ends the cycle of births and deaths, allowing the yogi freedom from the possibility of rebirth.

The influence of the philosophy of yoga has spread widely over the centuries, and elements of it have appeared in all of the main religions. The doctrine of karma and reincarnation is widely accepted in the East, and when birth and rebirth are seen as signs of pain and suffering, then death can be seen as a liberator, for all of humanity. According to the yoga traditon, the cycle of births and deaths may be broken while still in human form by the spirit of grace, and by concentrated will and devotion.

Out of ignorance man clings to life and to the pursuit of happiness, normally to find only pain and sorrow. The yogi on his long spiritual journey is not immune from suffering until he has attained the final liberation (while still incarnate), and there remains the possibility at any stage along the path of falling back and becoming victim to passion, desire, ignorance and attachment. It is not until the yogi has completely destroyed the seed of ignorance and become firmly established in *true* knowledge that he can be safe from the possibility of rebirth. Exceptions arise, however, when the yogi *chooses* to reincarnate in order to serve his fellow beings and assist them in reaching the goal of liberation.

Pure, unmodified knowledge is the essence of what *is,* not what might be, nor of anything that has been constructed by thought. It is beyond opinion, conjecture and speculation, because truth is absolute and transcends all human values. With the expansion of consciousness, the yogi leaves behind all limitations, turning irrevocably towards truth, and this knowledge is without modification.

Sūtra 3.19

कवर्गादिषु माहेश्वर्याद्याः पशुमातरः ।

kavargādiṣu māheśvaryādyāḥ paśu-mātaraḥ

The power of the Divine may find expression through the Great Lord Īśvara in sound (as in the Word), and through manifestation as the Mother of all beings.

This is a difficult sūtra, but it repays the effort to understand its meaning. The Creator of the universe is not to be anthropomorphized and given a male *or* a female epithet. The Divine Principle does, however, find expression through manifestation in a male or female *aspect.* The Great Lord Īśvara (Maheśvara, or Śiva) may be regarded as the male aspect, and finds expression in the hearts and minds of all men and women through the power of the Word (i.e., scripture and the sacred texts). The sound of the Word is potentially both creative and destructive, but it also has the power of transformation, in terms of human consciousness.

The Great Mother (Mātara) is not so much an opposing force as a complementary force, just as spirit and matter are dual aspects of the essential creative unity of existence. She has the ability to find resonance with the inner consciousness of all beings that have been born, *and* that have yet to be born. She is not separate from Maheśvara, but is one with Him in spirit, and is herself the Mother of all Creation. All beings within the field of saṃsāra are limited, and are normally unaware of their spiritual origins, but with effort and perseverance, each may find union with the Creator, who is ultimately both Mother and Lord of the Universe.

Sūtra 3.20

त्रिषु चतुर्थं तैलवदासेच्यम् ।

triṣu caturthaṃ tailavad-āsecyam

There is a fourth state of consciousness which goes beyond the other states of waking, dreaming and dreamless sleep.

The ordinary states of waking, dreaming and dreamless sleep can be enlightened and transformed by the fourth state of consciousness (turīya). In this state the everyday activities of thinking and being go beyond their normal limitations. Turīya is a state which permeates the other three states, by lifting them beyond their limits of awareness and their domination by sensory experience. The inner awareness needs to be experienced continually, and not simply during moments of recollection. In other words, it does not arise from thought, reasoning or trance-like states of consciousness. Rather it arises from one-pointedness and dedication towards truth and understanding. This attribute becomes part of the consciousness of the yogi through constant meditation and devotion towards the Inner Self.[30]

Sūtra 3.21

मग्नः स्वचित्तेन प्रविशेत् ।

magnaḥ svacittena praviśet

The fourth state entered into by immersion in the inner consciousness is marked by clarity of understanding.

Turīya is a state of consciousness, and there has to be a mind-center to experience it. This mind-center exists within every human being, although its expression is normally limited by thought and the ordinary states of consciousness. If these states can be illumined by a clarity of purpose and understanding, then the yogi can function at the higher level at any time he chooses. Turīya is experienced *through* the ordinary states of conscious-

30. viz. *Śiva Sūtras 1:11*.

ness and not outside of them. Waking, sleeping and dreaming states continue to exist, but no longer as conditioned existence, dominated by the processes of thought. These states will never penetrate the mysteries of existence without the illumination which comes from within, transcending all ordinary existence.

Sūtra 3.22

प्राणसमाचारे समदर्शनम् ।

prāṇa-samācāre sama-darśanam

When the fourth state of consciousness has been attained, the forces of prāṇa are held in control, and there follows an awareness of the unity of all existence.

The forces of prāṇa are the vital forces which sustain all living beings. Prāṇa represents not so much the physical breath as the vitality of kuṇḍalinī, the serpent power which rises up from the base of the spine and spirals around the spinal cord. It is said that the central channel of suṣumṇā is awakened in "turīya consciousness." This awakening will affect the flow of subtle energies around the body, and also lead to singleness of purpose and to freedom from the pairs of opposites (between which one is normally prone to oscillate). Integration of mind, body and spirit is frequently referred to in spiritual philosophy, and here it becomes a reality.

When all the energies of the body are pulling in the same

direction there is an increase in vitality and a greater ability to perform tasks that are set before us. This state of equipoise or equilibrium can be sensed by others who are "aware," and these others may be taken to include physical and nonphysical beings who respond to a particular keynote and create vibrations in the higher spheres. One should remember that higher spheres are not "somewhere else," but exist on a higher frequency, at a superphysical level, and are associated with the spiritual luminosity. The identity of these superphysical beings is a subject of consideration outside the present context; I merely state that working together in harmony need not be limited to the spiritual dimensions of man alone.

Sūtra 3.23

मध्येऽवरप्रसवः ।

madhye'vara-prasavaḥ

Attainment of the fourth state may not be complete, as impressions from the mind arise in the intervening period.

The mind is always a potential obstacle in the process of enlightenment, and when turīya is first experienced there will be periods of ordinary thought activity which intervene while functioning in the other states of consciousness. This continues until the point is reached where absorption is complete and impressions from the mind cease to arise. The intervening periods eventually cease to occur; this process is like the meditation technique whereby a seed thought is held in the mind, and then there is a brief moment between one thought fading and another one entering the mind. This moment is the "seed" of silence, and stillness of mind, and it begins as just a flash. This can gradually be expanded until the mind is completely still, and a continual state of bliss is experienced.

Sūtra 3.24

मात्रास्वप्रत्ययसंधाने नष्टस्य
पुनरुत्थानम् ।

mātrā-svapratyaya-saṃdhāne naṣṭasya punar-utthānam

The higher state of consciousness (turīya) is regained by persistent effort towards the realization of the Higher Self.

Patanjali speaks of one-pointed dedication to Īśvara in the *Yoga Sūtras*,[31] and other great teachers have reiterated the ancient truth that by absolute dedication, and single-mindedness towards the ultimate goal of Self-realization (union with the Divine), the state of spiritual union can be attained. In this state of consciousness the impressions received during periods of non-absorption with the Divine are transcended, and the turīya state is attained.

31. viz. *Yoga Sūtras 1:23–29*.

This vision provides a goal for the aspiring yogi, as he or she struggles to free the mind from domination by the senses and from the limitations of the ordinary states of consciousness. Continuous devotion and persistent effort are the characteristics needed for the accomplishment of this goal.

Sūtra 3.25

शिवतुल्यो जायते ।

śivatulyo jāyate

He who achieves Self-realization becomes as one with Śiva.

While the yogi, functioning in the world of manifestation, directs his will towards Self-realization (i.e., Union with the Divine), his consciousness becomes slowly absorbed with that of the Lord Śiva. Therefore, one-pointed dedication to Īśvara or Śiva which arises from persistent effort leads irrevocably towards Union, Liberation and realization of the nature of the Divine within.

Sūtra 3.26

शरीरवृत्तिर्व्रतम् ।

śarīra-vṛttir-vratam

To him who has achieved Self-realization, retaining a physical body is an act of devotion.

Freedom from the cycle of birth and rebirth is an accomplishment which the yogi may seek to achieve, but as in the Buddhist tradition of the bodhisattva, the greatest sacrifice is made when the enlightened one *chooses* to retain a physical body in order to serve humanity. This is described as an act of devotion, when the pursuit of personal freedom and bliss is exchanged for the hardship and limitations of a physical body. Suffering is an inescapable fact of life, but there is no better way to relieve the burden of karma (individual or collective) than to strive to relieve the suffering of other human beings (which is hard to accomplish without the vehicle of a physical body). The yogi may regard it as a privilege to occupy a physical body, and by conducting a pure life and by serving the "highest cause" he is assisting, in some small measure, in the process of divine evolution.

Sūtra 3.27

कथा जपः ।

kathā japaḥ

His conversation (reflects the state of Self-realization) and has the character of a prayer.

In this state of Self-awareness, ordinary conversation rises above the mundane and assumes the importance of a "religious discourse," and when consciousness has been transformed, the individual characteristics of speech are said to assume the nature of a prayer. Conversation for one who is in the state of turīya has the nature and property of a religious discourse, because the mind of the yogi is tuned to the Inner Self (ātmā).

Sūtra 3.28

दानमात्मज्ञानम् ।

dānam-ātma-jñānam

The gift of Self-knowledge may be offered to one who seeks to know.

The virtue of charity is extolled by all religions, and the gift of wisdom is something of great value. As such, it cannot be given, only communicated, and then not by words, but by understanding. The yogi who treads the Path is often compelled from within to show others the way. It is within his powers to offer that gift, the essence of which is not ordinary knowledge, but wisdom and compassion. The yogi, or guru, may help in opening the spiritual centers in another by hidden means, and enable the sādhaka to progress beyond previous limitations. However, the yogi can only *show* the way, because it will not benefit the pupil if the teacher undertakes the journey on his behalf. It is the pupil that must make the effort in order to reach the goal, in the same way as when a physician prescribes a remedy, but gives it to the patient to take.

Sūtra 3.29

योऽविपस्थो ज्ञाहेतुश्च ।

yo'vipastho jñāhetuś-ca

He (the yogi) also has the power to act as an instrument of Self-knowledge.

One function of the yogi is to act as a facilitator; in other words, while he may teach his pupil and show him the way, the yogi may also provide the stimulus for spiritual growth. The source from which the yogi finds inspiration is the same source which acts as a catalyst for change in the pupil. Self-knowledge, or wisdom, provides the object of attainment, and the torch of true knowledge will not be passed on unless the spirit of ātmā burns within.

True knowledge is both difficult to comprehend, and to express through the written word. To some extent esoteric knowledge has built-in safeguards, because by its nature it holds little attraction for the casual inquirer. On the other hand, persistent effort, supported by the light of understanding, *is* a means of attainment, and in this situation the yogi has an important role to perform as the instrument or facilitator of Self-knowledge.

Sūtra 3.30

स्वशक्तिप्रचयोऽस्य विश्वम् ।

svaśakti-pracayo'sya viśvam

From true knowledge of the Self arises the power to create an entire universe.

From Self-mastery arises Self-knowledge, and from Self-knowledge arises understanding of the true nature of Reality. This knowledge is power, and this power, or śakti, is without limitation when the consciousness of the yogi is united with that of Śiva. Ultimately, it must be remembered, Śiva is the Creator, Preserver and Destroyer of the universe and is the essence of Divine Will, without which nothing that is *is*. Śiva, or Īśvara, is the Lord of all creation, and all manifestation is in turn an expression of His Consciousness.

Even at the mundane level, knowledge bestows responsibility and power on one who has attained it. How much greater is the responsibility, therefore, when such knowledge is the true knowledge of the nature of Reality, which can be expanded to the extent of being able to create a complete manifested system. Gross objects and ordinary consciousness have their limitations, but true Self-knowledge is of an entirely different order, being infinite in power and without limitation.

Sūtra 3.31

स्थितिलयौ ।

sthiti-layau

This power extends to the maintenance and reabsorption of the manifested universe.

This is an amplification and extension of the previous sūtra, insomuch as the śakti by which the universal system is manifest (as an expression of the Will of Śiva) extends to the maintenance or preservation of that system, and towards its eventual dissolution (or reabsorption into the unmanifested state).

The consciousness of the yogi is directed towards the union of consciousness with Śiva. This union creates a power which is the energy behind the whole creative process, with its phases of manifestation, maintenance and reabsorption (or creation, preservation and destruction). The final phase in the cycle involves the reintegration of the parts into the whole, which is the state of pure, undifferentiated consciousness. This describes the cyclic nature of the whole of existence, in which the processes of evolution function throughout space and time.

Sūtra 3.32

तत्प्रवृत्तावप्यनिरासः संवेतृभावात् ।

tat-pravṛttāvapyanirāsaḥ saṃvetṛ-bhāvāt

The yogi is continually aware, despite the changing states of manifestation in the universe.

It is said that the yogi can stand aside from the great "comings and goings" within the manifested system, by reason of his unity with the consciousness of Śiva. It is understood that the process of manifestation is an expression of the Will of Śiva. Therefore the creation, preservation and destruction of the universe is a process which unfolds through the power of the Divine Will. The yogi who has fixed his consciousness on the Will of Śiva has learnt to sustain conscious awareness by his own effort and perseverance. In this way he ceases to be affected by the constant changes within the system of manifestation, which in other people dominate the ordinary thinking process.

Sūtra 3.33

सुखासुखयोर्बहिर्मननम् ।

sukhāsukhayor-bahir-mananam

Pleasure and pain appear as external to the yogi, and do not touch the deeper levels of consciousness.

The ātmā is above all sensory experience, and the yogi has so developed his consciousness that he is able to direct it at will. He is capable of experiencing both pleasure and pain, but he does not identify them as belonging to the I-consciousness. Training and experience have taught him to assign them to their proper place, and not to allow emotional reactions to interfere with the identification of the Self with the ātmā. This process is accompanied by the practice of discrimination and Self-awareness, as the yogi observes his own daily actions. Sensory experience may be more intense than in the ordinary person, because of heightened sensitivity. However, the yogi does not allow domination of thought and consciousness by the emotions and the physical senses.

Sūtra 3.34

तद्विमुक्तस्तु केवली ।

tad-vimuktastu kevalī

The yogi who is free from the influence of pleasure and pain is centered in his own pure consciousness.

The pairs of opposites hold sway over most aspects of ordinary life, with karma holding the balance. Pleasure and pain are the most fundamental of the opposites and occupy the mind of everyone but the yogi, in the ordinary waking state (jāgrat). The yogi has learnt to detach himself from the influence of pleasure and pain and rests, by his own effort, in the seat of his own pure consciousness. Identification with the ātmā becomes total, and this leaves no room for the illusions of duality and subjective experience.

Sūtra 3.35

मोहप्रतिसंहतस्तु कर्मात्मा ।

moha-prati-saṃhatastu karmātmā

However, one who is bound by attachment to pleasure and pain is not free from karma and delusions (arising in the mind).

This sūtra describes the circumstances in which the mind is not freed from delusion, when fresh karma is generated by attachment to action on the physical plane and by the continued experience of pleasure and pain. Delusion is the inevitable consequence of this attachment. The mind cannot be pointed in different directions at once, and *attachment* to sensation precludes one-pointed dedication to spiritual union. Meditation on the Divine is thus obstructed by impressions from the mind, which may be caused by delusion and the attraction of the opposites, so characteristic of physical sensation.

Experience of pleasure and pain is important for the growth and development of the jīvātmā (soul), but can prevent the liberation which comes from the complete realization of the Self. The yogi has learnt detachment, and to free himself from the force of karma, having no need of further experiences for his own evolution.

Sūtra 3.36

भेदतिरस्कारे सर्गान्तरकर्मत्वम् ।

bheda-tiraskāre sargāntara-karmatvam

From the removal of the causes of attachment to pleasure and pain arises a different perception of Reality and the phenomenal world.

A point may be reached when a conscious decision is taken to turn away from the world of the senses and desire. It may take lifetimes to come to the point of making that decision, but when the surrender has been made, and the attachments broken, the change of consciousness can lead to a wholly new perception of life with regard to Reality and the phenomenal world. The sacrifices involved will bring their reward, not only in terms of changes in perception but in terms of waves of bliss and peace which may fill the whole being as obstacles to union with the Divine are removed.

The choices outlined in the commentary to the previous sūtra must be made without hindrance; if there is secret longing and resistance from within, turmoil may arise and disturb the balance of the mind. However, if the time is right, and the attachment to pleasure and pain is broken, then the change in perception alluded to in this sūtra will naturally arise. Pain is the downside of pleasure, and perhaps its inevitable corollary; however, they are not opposites, but *one,* like the two sides of a coin.

Sūtra 3.37

करणशक्तिः स्वतोऽनुभवात् ।

karaṇa-śaktiḥ svato'nubhavāt

The power of creativity arises naturally from within, when the union (of consciousness with the Divine) has been experienced (by the yogi).

To the ordinary person, the creative powers of the yogi may appear phenomenal, but an understanding of the nature of these powers will bring about the realization that they are essentially the workings of the universal laws of Nature. These laws are manifest in the phenomenal world, with all its intricate workings. It should not come as a surprise that the yogi has great powers of creativity, whether or not they have form in the ordinary manifested state. The essential prerequisite is the accomplishment of perfect union between the consciousness of Śiva and the yogi. When this state has been accomplished, no additional effort is required by the yogi to manifest these powers; they simply arise silently from within.

Sūtra 3.38

त्रिपदाद्यनुप्राणनम् ।

tripadādyanuprāṇanam

The lower three states of consciousness are enlivened by the fourth, in which lies the creative principle (or power of creativity).[32]

The nature of turīya, or the fourth state of consciousness, has previously been described, and it is within this state that the power of creativity lies hidden. The yogi has learnt to live in the fourth state of consciousness, having devoted effort to extend his awareness beyond the confines of the states of sleep, wakefulness and dreamless sleep. Turīya is akin to the meditative state in which the mind and the physical body are transcended and awareness touches the Inner Self (or the luminosity within). When consciousness is filled with the Inner Light it extends, through its own radiance, towards the Divine. In this state the power of creativity "resides," and there is conscious control over the fundamental elements of Nature.[33] Without the enlivening spirit by which the turīya state is known, the ordinary states of consciousness lack purpose and intent.

32. viz. *Śiva Sūtras 3:20–24.*

33. Note that the term "creativity" in yoga philosophy does not have any connotation with art or artistic expression. It pertains only to the ability to demonstrate control over the elements, in the manner that has been described.

Sūtra 3.39

चित्तथितिवच्छरीरकरणबाह्येषु ।

cittasthitivaccharīra-karaṇa-bāhyeṣu

The body, the sense organs and the external world should be enlivened in the same way as the mind.

The yogi who is absorbed in the inner state of contemplation is able to extend the sense of bliss to all aspects of his being, and not restrict the animating principle to the mind. Everything flows outward from his inner state of being, so that the senses, the physical body and every action are all filled with the same spirit of bliss. Inner peace is radiated in all directions and to all beings when the yogi is enlivened by the creative power contained within the state of turīya.[34]

34. The word "enlivened" used in the last two sūtras refers to a state of animation, but only in the sense that something is imbued with the breath of prāṇa and spiritual energy, not in the sense of pertaining to an emotional state.

Sūtra 3.40

अभिलाषाद् बहिर्गतिः संवाह्यस्य ।

abhilāṣād bahirgatiḥ saṃvāhyasya

The desire to function in the external world may remain after touching the deeper levels of consciousness.

Desire is an evolutionary force; it is a force for change, for action and self-development, and is a natural component in the make-up of an individual. Difficulties arise when that force is uncontrolled or wrongly directed, but that does not in itself make it evil. When desire is channeled in a spiritual direction, its own inner power may be employed as an emotional tool for self-development, and as the aspirant climbs the evolutionary spiral, the objects of desire become more refined and less focused on the separate self.

All the same, desire can still cause difficulties in terms of force and direction. Even in the higher stages of development, desire can change direction suddenly like the wind, and throw a person off course; this can have serious and far-reaching consequences. In the context of the yogi, situations may arise when an intense desire exists for some action at the physical level, which may be quite selfless in nature. The desire to help a fellow being in an hour of need will be without any thought of self, but desire for sensual experience, being of an entirely different nature, still needs to be restrained.

The yogi does not necessarily function in the turīya state of consciousness at all times, and impressions from the past can appear, as can sensory impressions in moments of inattention. However, his strength of will and his control over the inner workings of the mind offer great protection to prevent these impressions from touching the deeper levels of consciousness. For the aspirant, such protection may be less strong, and it is always necessary to be mindful of impressions strong enough to dominate the mind.

Sūtra 3.41

तदारूढप्रमितेस्तत्क्षयाज्जीवसंक्षयः ।

tadārūḍha-pramites-tatkṣayāj-jīva-saṃkṣayaḥ

All desire ceases when the yogi becomes established in the state of union and Self-realization (the will for repeated experience having been exhausted).

Desire is intensified by the will, and there is a natural tendency to crave for repeated experience. Just as oxygen enables fire to burn, so gradual submission of the will (to the lower state) has the effect of *increasing* desire, and the sādhaka must guard against lapses of resolve and the re-emergence of the binding power of sensory impressions. As the sādhaka constantly directs his will to the discovery and adoration of the spirit of the Divine (through Śiva), he will be ever less prone to the re-emergence of these impressions. They fade as they lose their intensity, and eventually disappear when they are overcome by the spirit of ātmā. The "supply of oxygen" is then extinguished by the establishment of Self-realization.

Sūtra 3.42

भूतकञ्चुकी तदा विमुक्तो भूयः
पतिसमः परः ।

bhūtakañcukī tadā vimukto bhūyaḥ
patisamaḥ paraḥ

The physical body is worn like a garment by one who is free from desire and who assumes the likeness of Śiva.

It is emphasized here that the physical body is a "covering of light" or a garment which clothes the ātmā (which is permanent and is unaffected by material circumstance). The yogi, having full knowledge of this, is able to use his body as a vehicle, without any attachment or emotional desire. Once he is free from the delusions of ignorance, hatred and desire, there is no longer any identification with sense impressions, and the liberated yogi becomes incapable of attachment to the outer shell or physical body (which is so often mistaken for the real Self).

Sūtra 3.43

नैसर्गिकः प्राणसंबन्धः ।

naisargikaḥ prāṇa-saṃbandhaḥ

Prāṇa is the link which animates the physical form with the principle of vital energy.

Prāṇa is the transmitter of energy from the causal plane to the physical plane of manifestation, and animates the physical form with the life-force (or principle of vital energy). The proper circulation of prāṇa around the body is important for good health, and so any obstruction, whether physical or subtle, to this flow of energy tends to lead to disease and ill-health after a period of time. (Acupuncture, for example, is an "energy medicine" which detects and treats either excess or insufficiency of vitality (prāṇa) in the different systems of the body. It works as an "interface" between the gross physical body and the subtle or superphysical form through the meridian system, which is a network of tiny ducts used to carry prāṇa, or "chi," around the body.)

Sūtra 3.44

नासिकान्तर्मध्यसंयमात्, किमत्र,
सव्यापसव्यसौषुम्नेषु ।

nāsikāntarmadhya-saṃyamāt kimatra savyāpasavya-sauṣumneṣu

Iḍā, piṅgalā and suṣumṇā are the three channels through which the vital force of prāṇa flows. The yogi regulates the breath and controls the central channel (suṣumṇā) by directing awareness to the seat of inner consciousness.[35]

The science of prāṇayama has long mystified the Westerner, having by nature a strong tendency towards analytical thought and empirical observation. The idea of directing breath through channels in the body is somewhat in opposition to orthodox or received "wisdom," with its mechanical approach to respiration and circulation. Even the *concept* of energy is foreign to many physicians, as too is the idea that centrally controlled (autonomic) nerve impulses can be overriden at will.[36]

It is paradoxical that the "modern" symbol of medicine is the caduceus, which depicts none other than iḍā, piṅgalā and the

35. viz. *Śiva Sūtras* 2:7.

36. The ancient Eastern mysteries are untouched by such skepticism, and the yogis have long guarded a body of knowledge in order to keep it "secure." These teachings have been given out at certain points in time, and the *Śiva Sūtras* are one such example.

controlling power of the serpent. Whilst the two outer channels direct the natural forces, suṣumṇā contains the kuṇḍalinī force, and is the main focus of attention in the present context. The sādhaka learns that controlled meditation on this channel will bestow the ability to employ prāṇa-śakti at will. This is not accomplished by exercising control of the breath, but by focusing awareness with one-pointed dedication on the Supreme Reality. The secret of prāṇa or vital force is demystified as it falls under the control of the will, in its state of apprehension of the Divine.

Sūtra 3.45

भूयः स्यात्प्रतिमीलनम् ।

bhūyaḥ syāt-pratimīlanam

Awareness of the unity of all existence will many times fill the consciousness of the yogi, which is inwardly and outwardly absorbed in the One Reality.

The consciousness of the yogi will only pass through limited modifications, as it is already directed towards the unity of all existence. As the result of previous efforts and inner spirituality, the yogi, who is dedicated towards the One Reality, will experience recurring moments of union in his own inner consciousness. These moments become more frequent and more intense as they expand and as the yogi becomes "inwardly and outwardly absorbed in the One Reality." The Inner Light has the power to cut through the many veils that surround the physical form, and this spiritual luminosity is the guiding light of the creative force of the Divine. When all modifications of the mind cease, then union with the Divine is unbroken, and this state of absorption is continuous when the yogi attains final Liberation.[37]

---

37. This is the state of kaivalya, described in Book Four of the *Yoga Sūtras*.

ओं नमः शिवायः

Oṃ namaḥ Śivāyaḥ

Bibliography

Translations of the *Śiva Sūtras*

Dyczkowski, Mark S. G. *The Aphorisms of Śiva: The* ŚivaSūtra *with Bhāskara's Commentary, the* Vārttika. Albany: State University of New York Press, 1992.

Singh, Jaideva. *Śiva Sūtras: The Yoga of Supreme Identity*. Delhi: Motilal Banarsidass, 1979.

Taimni, I. K. *The Ultimate Reality and Realization.* Adyar, India: Theosophical Publishing House, 1976.

Other Works

Dehejia, Harsha. *Parvatidarpana: An Exposition of Kaśmir Śaivism Through the Images of Śiva and Parvati.* Delhi: Motilal Banarsidass, 1997.

Dyczkowski, Mark. *The Doctrine of Vibration: An Analysis of the Doctrines and Practices of Kashmir Shaivism.* Albany: State University of New York Press, 1987.

Isayeva, Natalia. *From Early Vedanta to Kashmir Shaivism: Gaudapada, Bhartrhari, and Abhinavagupta.* Albany: State University of New York Press, 1995.

Lakshman Jee, Swami. *Kashmir Shaivism: The Secret Supreme.* Albany: State University of New York Press, 1988.

Muktananda, Swami. *Nothing Exists That Is Not Śiva: Commentaries on the Śiva Sūtra, Vijñānabhairava, Gurugītā, and Other Sacred Texts.* South Fallsburg, N.Y.: SYDA Foundation, 1997.

Muller-Ortega, Paul Eduardo. *The Triadic Heart of Śiva: Kaula Tantricism of Abhinavagupta in the Non-Dual Shaivism of Kashmir.* Albany: State University of New York Press, 1989.

Shastri, J. L., ed. *The Liṅga Purāṇas* [Ancient Indian Tradition and Mythology Series,Vols. 5–6]. Delhi: Motilal Banarsidass, 1973.

Siddhantashastree, Rabindra Kumar. *Śaivism Through the Ages*. Delhi: Munishiram Manoharlal, 1974.

Singh, Jaideva. *The Yoga of Vibration and Divine Pulsation: A Translation of the* Spanda Karikas *with Kṣemarāj's Commentary, the* Spanda Nirnaya. Delhi: Motilal Banarsidass, 1992.

Taimni, I. K. *The Science of Yoga*. Wheaton, Ill.: Theosophical Publishing House, 1961.

Taimni, I. K. *The Secret of Self-Realization: Pratyabhijñā Hridayam of Kṣemarāja*. Adyar, India: Theosophical Publishing House, 1974.

Worthington, Roger. *A Student's Companion to Patanjali*. London: Theosophical Publishing House, 1987.

RY

ion of consciousness,"
the Supreme Being

center for spiritual

., rāja yoga)

the Divine within

is enlightened

āveśa entering the body of another

avidyā ignorance, "not knowing"

bhāvanā the state of pure being

bhūta an element (as in nature)

bodhisattva one who chooses to reincarnate, after having attained kaivalya

Brahma the god of creation; the divine essence; the sacred Word; the first aspect of the Hindu Trinity

buddhi the faculty of mental perception

cakra a center or vortex pertaining to the physical form

cit mind, or mind principle

citta mind-consciousness

guṇa a characteristic of matter (i.e., its individual properties)

guru a spiritual teacher

icchā will, as in the will of Śakti

iḍā one of the three nāḍīs

indriyas the physical senses

Īśvara the Supreme Being, or god of the entire universe

jāgrat wakeful consciousness

japa repetition (as of a mantra); murmuring of prayers

jīvātmā the soul

jñāna knowledge or wisdom

kaivalya the state of final liberation

karma action (lit.); the law of cause and effect

kleśas obstacles on the path of yoga

kuṇḍalinī serpent power, or spiritual energy focused at the base of the spine

liṅga male symbol of fertility (phallus)

Mahābhārata the name of the great Indian epic poem

mahābindu the great point; the focus of meditation (non-spatially), between the mind state and the state of enlightenment or superconsciousness

Maheśvara a synonym for Īśvara or Śiva

manas mind, as the vehicle of thought

mantra a short prayer or invocation

māyā illusion, or unreality

nāḍī a channel for the circulation of subtle energy around the body (the three major channels being iḍā, piṅgalā and suṣumnā)

Naṭarāja the cosmic dancer

nirvāṇa the final release from the cycle of birth and rebirth

Oṃ the sacred syllable, or invocation to the divine

pañca the number five

pañcakṣari the five-syllabled mantra

para- the highest or supreme . . .

Parabrahman that which is beyond Brahma; that which is nameless; god

piṅgalā one of the three nāḍīs

pralaya silent rest, as between periods of activity, or manifestation

prāṇa breath, or vital energy

praṇava the sacred syllable Oṃ

prāṇayama systematic regulation of the breath

śabda sound, or word (as of sacred origin)

Śaivism the worship of Śiva; the religion devoted to Śiva

Śakti power (the feminine aspect); energy; that which complements Śiva

Śaktopāya "the book of the creative power within," or the realization of Śakti

Śāmbhavopāya "the book of Self-realization," or the realization of Śiva

śarīra vehicle or body

Śiva name of the Supreme Being; the third aspect of the Hindu Trinity

śloka verse or hymn

sādhaka an aspirant on the path to fulfillment

samādhi the state of illumination, as in meditation

saṃdhāna a state of union, or joining together, as in meditation

saṃsāra the ocean of worldly existence

sat being (existence)

sattva the state of balance or equilibrium

siddhi a psychic power

suṣumṇā the central channel through which the kundalini flows

suṣupti the state of dreamless sleep

sūtra an aphorism, or thread

svapna the dream state of consciousness

taṇḍava the cosmic dance of Śiva

tattva "thatness," or a principle of existence

turīya the fourth state of consciousness

vairāgya dispassion or desirelessness

vidya ordinary or scientific knowledgē sometimes translated as "wisdom"

Viṣṇu the god of preservation, or second aspect of the Hindu Trinity

viveka discrimination; true knowledge

yoga union (as between spirit and matter)

yogi one who is accomplished in the practices of yoga

yoni the female symbol of fertility (vulva)

INDEX

About Roger Worthington, Ph.D.

Roger Worthington, Ph.D., has studied Eastern philosophy for nearly thirty years, specializing in classical Indian philosophy, and in particular the philosophy of yoga. He practiced raja yoga over a long period, and has given classes in London.

His professional interest is in healthcare and ethics, which stemmed from when he worked as an osteopath in England. He obtained a master's degree in medical ethics from Keele University in England and has recently completed his doctorate in philosophy at the State University of New York at Buffalo. His dissertatin comprised an international study of healthcare and distributive justice.

He now lectures in medical law and ethics at St. George's Hospital in London.

The main building of the Institute headquarters, near Honesdale, Pennsylvania.

The Himalayan Institute

FOUNDED IN 1971 by Swami Rama, the Himalayan Institute has been dedicated to helping people grow physically, mentally, and spiritually by combining the best knowledge of both the East and the West.

Our international headquarters is located on a beautiful 400-acre campus in the rolling hills of the Pocono Mountains of northeastern Pennsylvania. The atmosphere here is one to foster growth, increased inner awareness, and calm. Our grounds provide a wonderfully peaceful and healthy setting for our seminars and extended programs. Students from around the world join us here to attend programs in such diverse areas as hatha yoga, meditation, stress reduction, Ayurveda, nutrition, Eastern philosophy, psychology, and other subjects. Whether the programs are for weekend meditation retreats, week-long seminars on spirituality, months-long residential programs, or holistic health services, the attempt here is to provide an environment of gentle inner progress.

We invite you to join with us in the ongoing process of personal growth and development.

The Institute is a nonprofit organization. Your membership in the Institute helps to support its programs. Please call or write for information on becoming a member.

Institute Programs, Services, and Facilities

Institute programs share an emphasis on conscious holistic living and personal self-development, including:

- Special weekend or extended seminars to teach skills and techniques for increasing your ability to be healthy and enjoy life
- Meditation retreats and advanced meditation and philosophical instruction
- Vegetarian cooking and nutritional training
- Hatha yoga workshops
- Hatha yoga teachers training
- Residential programs for self-development
- Holistic health services and Ayurvedic Rejuvenation Programs through the Institute's Center for Health and Healing.

A *Quarterly Guide to Programs and Other Offerings* is free within the USA. To request a copy, or for further information, call 800-822-4547 or 570-253-5551, fax 570-253-9078, email bqinfo@HimalayanInstitute.org, write the Himalayan Institute, RR 1 Box 1127, Honesdale, PA 18431-9706 USA, or visit our website at www.HimalayanInstitute.org.

The Himalayan Institute Press

THE HIMALAYAN INSTITUTE PRESS has long been regarded as "The Resource for Holistic Living." We publish dozens of titles, as well as audio and video tapes, that offer practical methods for living harmoniously and achieving inner balance. Our approach addresses the whole person—body, mind, and spirit—integrating the latest scientific knowledge with ancient healing and self-development techniques.

As such, we offer a wide array of titles on physical and psychological health and well-being, spiritual growth through meditation and other yogic practices, as well as translations of yogic scriptures.

Our yoga accessories include the Japa Kit for meditation practice, the Neti® Pot, the ideal tool for sinus and allergy sufferers, and The Breath Pillow®, a unique tool for learning health-supportive diaphragmatic breathing.

Subscriptions are available to a bimonthly magazine, *Yoga International,* which offers thought-provoking articles on all aspects of meditation and yoga, including yoga's sister science, Ayurveda.

For a free catalog call 800-822-4547 or 570-253-5551, email hibooks@HimalayanInstitute.org, fax 570-253-6360, write the Himalayan Institute Press, RR 1 Box 1129, Honesdale, PA 18431-9709, USA, or visit our website at www.HimalayanInstitute.org.